交通版高等学校交通工程专业规划教材

ENGLISH IN TRAFFIC ENGINEERING
交通工程专业英语

邬　岚　主　编
吴艳群　孙丽芳　林　丽　副主编
陈　峻　主　审

人民交通出版社股份有限公司
China Communications Press Co.,Ltd.

内 容 提 要

本书从交通运输类英语课程教学和研究的实际出发，将基础理论和专业英语的阅读、翻译以及专业论文的写作技巧相融合，分为三部分进行编写，第一部分为基础篇，介绍交通运输系统的功能、元素和主要问题；第二部分为专业篇，从现代交通工程所涉及的主要方面选编了热门题材且文字生动的文章；第三部分为技巧篇，从翻译技巧到专业论文的写作技巧进行了详细介绍。书后给出了练习的参考答案。

本书可作为高等院校交通工程专业、交通运输专业、土木工程专业及相关专业本科生的教材，也可作为科技工作者自学和科研的参考用书。

图书在版编目(CIP)数据

交通工程专业英语 / 邬岚主编.—北京：
人民交通出版社股份有限公司，2016.1
交通版高等学校交通工程专业规划教材
ISBN 978-7-114-12531-7

Ⅰ.①交… Ⅱ.①邬… Ⅲ.①交通工程 – 英语 – 高等学校 – 教材 Ⅳ.①H31

中国版本图书馆 CIP 数据核字(2015)第 243176 号

交通版高等学校交通工程专业规划教材

书　　名：	交通工程专业英语	
著 作 者：	邬　岚	
责任编辑：	富砚博　郭红蕊	
出版发行：	人民交通出版社股份有限公司	
地　　址：	(100011)北京市朝阳区安定门外外馆斜街3号	
网　　址：	http://www.ccpress.com.cn	
销售电话：	(010)59757973	
总 经 销：	人民交通出版社股份有限公司发行部	
经　　销：	各地新华书店	
印　　刷：	北京虎彩文化传播有限公司	
开　　本：	787×1092　1/16	
印　　张：	9.375	
字　　数：	220千	
版　　次：	2016年1月　第1版	
印　　次：	2024年1月　第4次印刷	
书　　号：	ISBN 978-7-114-12531-7	
印　　数：	6001—7000 册	
定　　价：	30.00元	

(有印刷、装订质量问题的图书由本公司负责调换)

交通版高等学校交通工程专业规划教材
编审委员会

主 任 委 员：徐建闽(华南理工大学)
副主任委员：马健霄(南京林业大学)
　　　　　　　王明生(石家庄铁道大学)
　　　　　　　王建军(长安大学)
　　　　　　　吴　芳(兰州交通大学)
　　　　　　　李淑庆(重庆交通大学)
　　　　　　　张卫华(合肥工业大学)
　　　　　　　陈　峻(东南大学)
委　　　员：马昌喜(兰州交通大学)
　　　　　　　王卫杰(南京工业大学)
　　　　　　　龙科军(长沙理工大学)
　　　　　　　朱成明(河南理工大学)
　　　　　　　刘廷新(山东交通学院)
　　　　　　　刘博航(石家庄铁道大学)
　　　　　　　杜胜品(武汉科技大学)
　　　　　　　郑长江(河海大学)
　　　　　　　胡启洲(南京理工大学)
　　　　　　　常玉林(江苏大学)
　　　　　　　梁国华(长安大学)
　　　　　　　蒋阳升(西南交通大学)
　　　　　　　蒋惠园(武汉理工大学)
　　　　　　　韩宝睿(南京林业大学)
　　　　　　　靳　露(山东科技大学)
秘 书 长：张征宇(人民交通出版社股份有限公司)

(按姓氏笔画排序)

前 言

从事技术工作的人常需要学习他人之所长,"借他山之石以攻玉"。英语这一全球工程技术界通用的语言可以帮助我们了解国内外同行的研究状态和技术水平,也有助于同行间的沟通与合作。中国城镇建设高速持续发展,国家对各类交通运输人才需求日增,对交通运输类高素质人才培养提出了新的要求,从而对交通运输类教材建设也提出了新的要求。本教材正是为了适应当今时代对高层次人才培养的需求而编写。

本教材从内容上体现出科学严谨性、理论实用性和工程技术创新性,以促进读者对现代交通工程的理解并获得启发,将所学的专业英语词汇和技术原理与原有的专业知识相互印证,启发新的技术方案,顺利查找英文技术资料,并开展课题的研究和论文的写作。

本书的编写体系有所创新。全书分为三篇,基础篇介绍背景知识,专业篇选取具有交通运输类特色的题材进行理论知识的加固,技巧篇介绍英语阅读时的翻译技巧并结合英语论文的写作结构、英文参考文献的写法及撰写规范等内容进行介绍。每章都围绕一个主题进行选材和编写,前两篇的基本内容包括2篇精读文章和1篇泛读课文,同时给出了专业词汇的释义以及相关的阅读理解和翻译的练习;第三篇在教学过程中,教师可依据需要选择文章进行精讲。本书题材选自国内外正式出版物,如学术专业著作、期刊等。参考了交通领域的相关时新内容,涵盖了交通工程专业各方面的基础理论,涉及交通流理论、交通控制、交通规划、交通安全、公共交通和智能交通技术等交通工程领域的内容。书后还提供了关于英文写作规范、常用的专业学术交流的网址,为读者检索查询国外资源以及进行规范的写作提供了平台。本书在编写过程中吸取了我国相近学科其他专业英语教材的优点和基础英语教学的经验,力求读者在有限学习时间中,了解现代交通工程专业的主要内容。

为帮助读者理解本书重点和难点内容,作者特制作了教学视频片段,读者可通过扫二维码"微课"下载学习。本书配套PPT课件,读者可登录人民交通出版社网站 http://www.ccpress.com.cn 或扫二维码"课件"免费下载。

微课　　课件

本书由南京林业大学邬岚主编,东南大学陈峻主审。编写人员如下:邬岚和兰州交通大学吴艳群编写第1、2章,东南大学叶智锐编写第3、6章,兰州交通大学孙丽芳编写第4、7章,其余章节由邬岚和林丽共同编写。本书编写过程中,研究生陈婷在整理资料与校对方面做了大量的工作,在此表示衷心的感谢!

限于编者的水平,书中不妥或错误之处在所难免,敬请读者不吝指正。

编 者
2015年10月

目 录

Part Ⅰ 基 础 篇

Chapter 1　Introduction to Traffic Engineering ········· 2
　Text A　Transportation Systems and Their Function ········· 2
　Text B　Elements of Traffic Engineering ········· 4
　Vocabulary and Glossary ········· 6
　Exercises ········· 7
　Reading Material：Traffic Engineering's Role and Objectives ········· 9
Chapter 2　Transportation System Issue ········· 13
　Text A　Traffic Problems and Challenges ········· 13
　Text B　Traffic Congestion and Congestion Pricing ········· 15
　Vocabulary and Glossary ········· 17
　Exercises ········· 18
　Reading Material：Ten-day Chinese Traffic Jam ········· 19

Part Ⅱ 专 业 篇

Chapter 3　Traffic Flow ········· 24
　Text A　Traffic Flow Parameters ········· 24
　Text B　Traffic Flow Theory ········· 26
　Vocabulary and Glossary ········· 30
　Exercises ········· 31
　Reading Material：Travel Time Studies ········· 32
Chapter 4　Traffic Control ········· 34
　Text A　Introduction to Traffic Control ········· 34
　Text B　Road Traffic Control ········· 36
　Vocabulary and Glossary ········· 41

  Exercises ·· 42
  Reading Material: Traffic Signal Control Systems ································· 43
Chapter 5 Traffic Planning ·· 48
  Text A What Will Our Community Look Like in the Future? ·············· 48
  Text B What Are the Travel Patterns in the Future? ··························· 50
  Vocabulary and Glossary ··· 55
  Exercises ·· 56
  Reading Material: Why are Planning Models Important? ······················· 57
Chapter 6 Traffic Safety ·· 60
  Text A Introduction to Traffic Safety ·· 60
  Text B Human Factors and Traffic Safety ······································· 61
  Vocabulary and Glossary ··· 63
  Exercises ·· 64
  Reading Material: Measures to Improve Traffic Safety ·························· 66
Chapter 7 Public Transportation ·· 68
  Text A History of Public Transportation ··· 68
  Text B Dial-A-Ride ··· 70
  Vocabulary and Glossary ··· 72
  Exercises ·· 72
  Reading Material: Carpooling ·· 73
Chapter 8 Intelligent Transportation System ··· 76
  Text A Advanced Traveler Information Systems ································ 76
  Text B Electronic Toll and Vehicle Classification ······························· 78
  Vocabulary and Glossary ··· 80
  Exercises ·· 81
  Reading Material: Applying ITS Technologies to TDM ························· 83

Part Ⅲ 技 巧 篇

翻译技巧 ·· 88
 技巧一:词类的转译 ·· 88
 技巧二:被动句的译法 ·· 90
 技巧三:省译与增译 ·· 95
 技巧四:长句的译法 ·· 101
 技巧五:数字的译法 ·· 102
论文写作技巧 ·· 106
 技巧六:语法技巧 ·· 106
 技巧七:论文的题目与作者 ·· 109

技巧八：摘要与关键词 ………………………………………………………… 110
技巧九：论文主体 ……………………………………………………………… 115
技巧十：英文参考文献的写法 ………………………………………………… 119
技巧十一：论文撰写规范 ……………………………………………………… 121

Key to Exercises …………………………………………………………………… 126
  Part I ……………………………………………………………………………… 126
    Chapter 1 …………………………………………………………………… 126
    Chapter 2 …………………………………………………………………… 126
  Part II ……………………………………………………………………………… 127
    Chapter 3 …………………………………………………………………… 127
    Chapter 4 …………………………………………………………………… 127
    Chapter 5 …………………………………………………………………… 128
    Chapter 6 …………………………………………………………………… 129
    Chapter 7 …………………………………………………………………… 129
    Chapter 8 …………………………………………………………………… 130

参考文献 ……………………………………………………………………………… 131

附录：交通专业英语网址选编 ……………………………………………………… 134

索引 …………………………………………………………………………………… 135

Part I

基础篇

Chapter 1　Introduction to Traffic Engineering

➔ Text A　Transportation Systems and Their Function

Transportation systems are a major component of economy and have an enormous impact on the shape of the society and the efficiency of the economy in general.

This growth pattern is one of the fundamental problems to be faced by traffic engineers. Given the relative maturity of our highway systems and the difficulty faced in trying to add system capacity, particularly in urban areas, the continued growth in vehicle-miles traveled leads directly to increased congestion on our highways. The inability to simply build additional capacity to meet the growing demand creates the need to address alternative modes, fundamental alterations in demand patterns, and management of the system to produce optimal results.

The Nature of Transportation Demand

Transportation demand is directly related to land-use patterns and to available transportation systems and facilities. Figure1.1 illustrates the fundamental relationship, which is circular and ongoing. Transportation demand is generated by the types, amounts, and intensity of land use, as well as its location. The daily journey to work, for example, is dictated by the locations of the worker's residence and employer and the times that the worker is on duty.

Transportation planners and traffic engineers attempt to provide capacity for observed or predicted travel demand by building transportation systems. The improvement of transportation systems, however, makes the adjacent and nearby lands more accessible and, therefore, more attractive for development. Thus, building new transportation facilities leads to further increases in land-use development, which (in turn) results in even higher transportation demands. This circular, self-reinforcing characteristic of traffic demand creates a central dilemma: build-

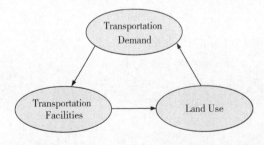

Figure 1.1　The Nature of Transportation Demand

ing additional transportation capacity invariably leads to incrementally increased travel demands.

On the other hand, demand is not constrained by capacity in all cities, and the normal process of attempting to accommodate demand as it increases is feasible in these areas. At the same time, the circular nature of the travel demand relationship will lead to congestion if care is not taken to manage both capacity and demand to keep them within tolerable limits.

If anything, we still tend to underestimate the impact of transportation facilities on land-use development. Often, the increase in demand is hastened by development occurring simply as a result of the planning of a new facility.

Concepts of Mobility and Accessibility

Transportation systems provide the nation's population with both mobility and accessibility. The two concepts are strongly interrelated but have distinctly different elements. Mobility refers to the ability to travel to many different destinations, while accessibility refers to the ability to gain entry to a particular site or area.

Mobility gives travelers a wide range of choices as to where to go to satisfy particular needs. Mobility allows shoppers to choose from among many competing shopping centers and stores. Similarly, mobility provides the traveler with many choices for all kinds of trip purposes, including recreational trips, medical trips, educational trips, and even the commute to work. The range of available choices is enabled by having an effective transportation network that connects to many alternative trip destinations within a reasonable time, with relative ease, and at reasonable cost.

Accessibility is a major factor in the value of land. When land can be accessed by many travelers from many potential origins, it is more desirable for development and, therefor, more valuable. Thus, proximity of land to major highways and public transportation facilities is a major factor determining its value.

Mobility and accessibility may also refer to different portions of a typical trip. Mobility focuses on the through portion of trips and is most affected by the effectiveness of through facilities that take a traveler from one general area to another. Accessibility requires the ability to make a transfer from the transportation system to the particular land parcel on which the desired activity is taking place. Accessibility, therefore, relies heavily on transfer facilities, which include parking for vehicles, public transit stops, and loading zones.

A good transportation system must provide for both mobility and accessibility and should be designed to separate the functions to the extent possible to ensure both safety and efficiency.

People, Goods, and Vehicles

The most common unit used by the traffic engineer is "vehicles." Highway systems are planned, designed, and operated to more vehicles safely and efficiently from place to place. Yet the movement of vehicles is not the objective, the goal is the movement of the people and goods that occupy vehicles.

Modern traffic engineering now focuses more on people and goods. While lanes must be added to a freeway to increase its capacity to carry vehicles, its person-capacity can be increased by increasing the average vehicle occupancy.

The efficient movement of goods is also vital to the general economy of the nation. The benefits of centralized and specialized production of various products are possible only if raw materials can be efficiently shipped to manufacturing sites and finished products can be efficiently distributed throughout the nation and the world for consumption. While long-distance shipment of goods and raw materials is often accomplished by water, rail, or air transportation, the final leg of the trip to deliver a good to the local store or the home of an individual consumer generally takes place on a truck using the highway system, part of the accessibility function is the provision of facilities that allow trucks to be loaded and unloaded with minimal disruption to through traffic and the accessibility of people to a given site.

The medium of all highway transportation is the vehicle. The design, operation, and control of highway systems relies heavily on the characteristics of the vehicle and of the driver. In the final analysis, however, the objective is to move people and goods, not vehicles.

Transportation Modes

While the traffic engineer deals primarily with highways and highway vehicles, there are other important transportation systems that must be integrated into a cohesive national, regional, and local transportation network.

The traffic engineer deals with all of these modes in a number of ways. All over-the-road modes-automobile, bus transit, trucking—are principal users of highway systems. Highway access to rail and air terminals is critical to their effectiveness, as is the design of specific transfer facilities for both people and freight. General access, internal circulation, parking, pedestrian areas, and terminals for both people and freight are all projects requiring the expertise of the traffic engineer.

Moreover, the effective integration of multimodal transportation systems is a major goal in maximizing efficiency and minimizing costs associated with all forms of travel.

Text B Elements of Traffic Engineering

Transportation engineering is the application of technology and scientific principles to the planning, functional design, operation, and management of facilities for any mode of transportation in order to provide for the safe, rapid, comfortable, convenient, economical, and environmentally compatible movement of people and goods.

Traffic engineering is that phase of transportation engineering which deals with the planning, geometric design and traffic operations of roads, streets, and highways, their networks, terminals, abutting lands, and relationships with other modes of transportation.

The objective of this course is to introduce traffic engineering fundamentals for highways and freeways to students.

The principal goal of the traffic engineer remains the provision of a safe system for highway traffic.

The objective of safe travelling comes the first and is never finished for the traffic engineer.

While speed of travel is much to be desired, it is limited by transportation technology, human characteristics, and the need to provide safety.

Comfort and convenience are generic terms and perceived differently by passengers. Comfort involves the physical characteristics of vehicles and roadways, and is influenced by our perception of safety. Convenience relates more to the ease with which trips are made and the ability of transport systems to accommodate all of our travel needs at appropriate times.

Cost is also relative. There is little in modern transportation systems that can be termed "cheap". Highway and other transportation systems involve massive construction, maintenance, and operating expenditures, most of which are provided through general and user taxes and fees. Nevertheless, every engineer, regardless of discipline, is called upon to provide the better systems at less cost.

Harmony with the environment is a complex issue that has become more important over time. All transportation systems have some negative impacts on the environment. All produce air and noise pollution in some forms, and all utilize valuable land resources.

There are a number of key elements of traffic engineering:

1. Traffic studies and characteristics;
2. Performance evaluation;
3. Facility design;
4. Traffic control;
5. Traffic operations;
6. Transportation systems management;
7. Integration of intelligent transportation system technologies.

Traffic studies and characteristics involve measuring and quantifying various aspect of highway traffic. Studies focus on data collection and analysis that is used to characterize traffic, including (but not limited to) traffic volumes and demands, speed and travel time, delay, accidents, origins and destinations, modal use, and other variables.

Performance evaluation is a means by which traffic engineers can rate the operating characteristics of individual sections of facilities and facilities as a whole in relative terms. Such evaluation relies on measures of performance quality and is often stated in terms of "levels of service". Levels of service are letter grades, from A to F, describing how well a facility is operating using specified performance criteria. Like grades in a course, A is very good, while F connotes failure (on some level). As part of performance evaluation, the capacity of highway facilities must be determined.

Facility design involves in the functional and geometric design of highways and other traffic facilities. Traffic engineers, per se, are not involved in the structural design of highway facilities but should have some appreciation for structural characteristics of their facilities.

Traffic control is a central function of traffic engineers and involve the establishment of traffic regulations and their communication to the driver through the use of traffic control devices, such as signs, markings, and signals.

Traffic operations involve measures that influence overall operation of traffic facilities, such as one-way street systems, transit operations, curb management, and surveillance and network control systems.

Transportation systems management (TSM) involves virtually all aspects of traffic engineering in a focus on optimizing system capacity and operations. Specific aspects of TSM include high-occupancy vehicle priority systems, car-pooling programs, pricing strategies to manage demand, and similar functions.

Intelligent transportation systems (ITS) refers to the application of modern telecommunications technology to the operation and control of transportation systems. Such systems include automated highways, automated toll-collection systems, vehicle-tracking systems, in-vehicle GPS and mapping systems, automated enforcement of traffic lights and speed laws, smart control devices, and others. This is a rapidly emerging family of technologies with the potential to radically alter the way we travel as well as the way in which transportation professionals gather information and control facilities. While the technology continues to expand, society will grapple with the substantial "big brother" issues that such systems invariably create.

This text contains material related to all of these components of the broad and complex profession of traffic engineering.

Vocabulary and Glossary

1. accessibility n. ①可及性②可达性;易接近;可亲
2. commute vi. 通勤
3. dilemma n. ①(进退两难的)困境,(左右为难的)窘境,进退维谷②任何一种窘境(或困境),(似乎无法解决的)难题③[逻辑学]两刀论法,二难推理,假言选言推理
4. freight vt. 运送;装货;使充满 n. 货运;运费;船货
5. highway n. 公路的统称,既可指高速公路,也可指一般道路
6. incrementally adv. 递增地;增值地
7. maturity n. ①成熟,完善,准备好②(票据的)到期,到期日,期限③[地质学]壮年(期)④[生物学]成熟期,发身期
8. mobility n. 移动性;机动性
9. per se adv. 本身;自身
10. proximity n. 亲近,接近

11. air terminal　航空集散站
12. automated toll-collection systems　自动收费系统
13. average vehicle occupancy　平均车辆占有率
14. facility design　设施设计
15. geometric design　几何设计；线形设计
16. highway system　公路系统
17. intelligent transportation systems（ITS）　智能交通系统
18. in-vehicle GPS and mapping systems　车载全球定位和地图系统
19. land parcel　地块；一块土地
20. land-use patterns　土地利用模式
21. levels of service　服务水平，简称 LOS
22. multimodal transportation systems　多方式交通运输系统
23. one-way street　单行道
24. pedestrian area　行人专区；步行街
25. raw materials　原料；原材料
26. self-reinforcing　自我强化；自我加强；自增强
27. structural design　结构设计
28. traffic and transportation　（微观的）交通和（宏观的）交通
29. traffic control　交通控制
30. traffic regulations　交通规则
31. traffic volume　交通量
32. transit stops　公共交通车站
33. transportation demand　交通需求
34. transportation facilities　运输设备；运输设施；运输工具
35. transportation mode　运输方式；交通方式
36. transportation planner　交通规划师
37. transportation systems management（TSM）　交通系统管理
38. vehicle-tracking systems　车辆追踪系统

Exercises

I. True or false.

1. Transportation demand is directly related to land-use patterns and to available transportation systems and facilities.　　　　　　　　　　　　　　　　　　　　　　　　　　（　　）

2. Transportation systems provide the nation's population with both mobility and inaccessibility.　　　　　　　　　　　　　　　　　　　　　　　　　　　　　　　　　　　（　　）

3. The most common unit used by the traffic engineer is "vehicles".　　　（　　）

4. Highways access to rail and air terminals is critical to their effectiveness, as is the design of specific transfer facilities for both people and freight. (　　)

5. Intelligent transportation system (ITS) refers to the application of modern telecommunications technology to the management and control of transportation systems. (　　)

II. Choose the best word or phrase to complete each statement.

1. Transportation systems are a major _____ of economy and have an enormous impact on the shape of the society and the efficiency of the economy in general.
   A. parts　　　　B. unit　　　　C. component　　　　D. assembly

2. Transportation demand is generated by the types, amounts, and _____ of land use, as well as its location.
   A. strength　　　B. intensity　　C. intension　　　　D. superiority

3. Mobility refers to the ability to travel to many different _____, while accessibility refers to the ability to gain entry to a particular site or area.
   A. destinations　B. goals　　　　C. fields　　　　　D. targets

4. Modern traffic engineering now _____ more on people and goods.
   A. emphasizes　　B. focuses　　　C. stress　　　　　D. underlines

5. While the technology continues to expand, society will _____ with the substantial "big brother" issues that such systems invariably create.
   A. grasp　　　　B. capture　　　C. collect　　　　D. grapple

III. Translate the following sentences into Chinese.

1. Similarly, mobility provides the traveler with many choices for all kinds of trip purposes, including recreational trips, medical trips, educational trips, and even the commute to work.

2. Yet the movement of vehicles is not the objective, the goal is the movement of the people and goods that occupy vehicles.

3. Studies focus on data collection and analysis that is used to characterize traffic, including (but not limited to) traffic volumes and demands, speed and travel time, delay, accidents, origins and destinations, modal use, and other variables.

4. Moreover, the effective integration of multimodal transportation systems is a major goal in maximizing efficiency and minimizing costs associated with all forms of travel.

5. Specific aspects of TSM include high-occupancy vehicle priority systems, car-pooling programs, pricing strategies to manage demand, and similar functions.

IV. Discussions.

1. What is the difference between mobility and accessibility?

2. Intelligent Traffic System (ITS) is the developing trend of future traffic. What is ITS?

Reading Material: Traffic Engineering's Role and Objectives

Introduction

Multi Protocol Label Switching (MPLS) is today mostly used for traffic engineering therefore we start by describing what traffic engineering is and why traffic engineering is needed.

Traffic engineering and fast reroute are the two major applications of constraint based routing. Traffic engineering is the process of controlling how traffic flows through a service provider's network so as to optimize resource utilization and network performance. Traffic engineering is needed in the Internet mainly because the shortest path is used in current intra-domain routing protocols (e. g. , OSPF, IS-IS) to forward traffic. The shortest path routing may give rise to two problems.

First, the shortest paths from different sources overlap at some links, resulting in congestion at those links.

Second, at some time, the traffic volume from a source to a destination could exceed the capacity of the shortest path, while a longer path between these two nodes remains under-utilized. The reason why conventional IP routing cannot provide traffic engineering is that it does not take into account the available bandwidth on individual links. For the purpose of traffic engineering, constraint based routing is used to route traffic trunk, which is defined as a collection of individual transmission control protocol (TCP), or user datagram protocol (UDP) flows, called "microflows" that share two common properties.

The first property is that all microflows are forwarded along the same common path.

The second property is that they all share the same class of service. By routing at the granularity traffic trunks, traffic trunks have better scaling properties than routing at the granularity of individual microflows with respect to the amount of forwarding state and the volume of control traffic.

In a sense, IP networks manage themselves. A host using the Transmission Control Protocol (TCP) adjusts its sending rate according to the available bandwidth on the path to the receiver. If the network topology should change, routers react to changes and calculate new paths to the destination. This has made the TCP/IP Internet a robust communication network. But robustness does not implicate that the network runs efficiently. The interior gateway protocols used today like OSPF and ISIS compute the shortest way to the destination and routers forward traffic according to the routing tables build from those calculations. This means that traffic from different sources passing through a router with the same destination will be aggregated and sent through the same path. Therefore a link may be congested despite the presence of under-utilized link in the network. And delay sensitive traffic like voice-over-IP calls may travel over a path with high propagation delay because this is the shortest path while a low latency path is available.

As illustrated in the above Figure 1.2 the shortest path from router 1 to 5 is the path (1-3-5).

All traffic passing through router 1 with destination router 5 (or another router with router 5 in the shortest path) will travel through this shortest path if the shortest path algorithm is used for forwarding in this network. Although there is an alternative path (1-2-4-5) available that could be used to distribute traffic more evenly in the network.

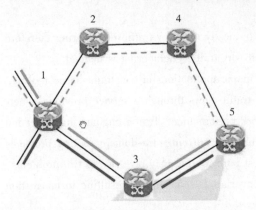

Figure 1.2 Traffic engineering

Traffic engineering is the process of controlling how traffic flows through a network to optimize resource utilization and network performance. Traffic engineering is basically concerned with two problems that occur from routing protocols that only use the shortest path as constraint when they construct a routing table.

The shortest paths from different sources overlap at some links, causing congestion on those links. The traffic from a source to a destination exceeds the capacity of the shortest path, while a longer path between these two routers is under-utilized.

MPLS can be used as a traffic engineering tool to direct traffic in a network in a more efficient way then original IP shortest path routing. MPLS can be used to control which paths traffic travels through the network and therefore a more efficient use of the network resources can be achieved. Paths in the network can be reserved for traffic that is sensitive, and links and router that is more secure and not known to fail can be used for this kind of traffic.

Traffic engineering's role in next-generation networks

Traditional service provider networks provided Layer 2 point-to-point virtual circuits with contractually predefined bandwidth. Regardless of the technology used to implement the service (X.25, Frame Relay or ATM), the trafficengineering (optimal distribution of load across all available network links) was inherent in the process.

In most cases, the calculation of the optimum routing of virtual circuits was done off-line by a network management platform; advanced networks (offering Frame Relay or ATM switched virtual circuits) also offered real-time on-demand establishment of virtual circuits. However, the process was always the same:

- The free network capacity was examined.
- The end-to-end or hop-by-hop path throughout the network that satisfied the contractual requirements (and, if needed, met other criteria) was computed.
- A virtual circuit was established along the computed path.

Internet and most IP-based services, including IP-based virtual private networks (VPNs) implemented with MPLS VPN, IPsec or Layer 2 transport protocol (L2TP), follow a completely different service model:

- The traffic contract specifies ingress and egress bandwidth for each site, not site-to-site traffic requirements.
- Every IP packet is routed through the network independently, and every router in the path makes independent next-hop decisions.
- Once merged, all packets toward the same destination take the same path (whereas multiple virtual circuits toward the same site could traverse different links).

Simplified to the extreme, the two paradigms could be expressed as follows:
- Layer 2 switched networks assume that the bandwidth is expensive and try to optimize its usage, resulting in complex circuit setup mechanisms and expensive switching methods.
- IP networks assume that the bandwidth is "free" and focus on low-cost, high-speed switching of a high volume of traffic.

The significant difference between the cost-per-switched-megabit of Layer 2 network (for example, ATM) and routed (IP) network has forced nearly all service providers to build next-generation networks exclusively on IP. Even in modern fiber-optics networks, however, bandwidth is not totally free, and there are always scenarios where you could use free resources of an underutilized link to ease the pressure on an overloaded path. Effectively, you would need traffic engineering capabilities in routed IP networks, but they are simply not available in the traditional hop-by-hop, destination-only routing model that most IP networks use.

Various approaches (including creative designs, as well as new technologies) have been tried to bring the traffic engineering capabilities to IP-based networks. We can group them roughly into these categories:
- The network core uses Layer 2 switched technology (ATM or Frame Relay) that has inherent traffic engineering capabilities. Virtual circuits are then established between edge routers as needed.
- IP routing tricks are used to modify the operation of IP routing protocols, resulting in adjustments to the path the packets are taking through the network.
- Deployment of IP-based virtual circuit technologies, including IP-over-IP tunnels and MPLS traffic engineering.

The Layer 2 network core design was used extensively when the service providers were introducing IP as an additional service into their WAN networks. Many large service providers have already dropped this approach because it does not result in the cost reduction or increase in switching speed that pure IP-based networks bring.

Traffic engineering objectives

Traffic Engineering (TE) is concerned with performance optimization of operational networks. More formally speaking, the key traffic engineering objectives are:

Minimizing congestion: Congestion occurs either when network resources are insufficient or inadequate to accommodate offered load or if traffic streams are inefficiently mapped onto available resources; causing subsets of network resources to become over-utilized while others remain underutilized.

Reliable network operations: Adequate capacity for service restoration must be available keeping in mind multiple failure scenarios, and at the same time, there must be mechanisms to efficiently and speedily reroute traffic through the redundant capacity. On recovering from the faults, re-optimization may be necessary to include the restored capacity.

Quality of Service requirements: In a multi-class service environment, where traffic streams with different service requirements contend with each other, the role of traffic engineering becomes more decisive. In such scenarios, traffic engineering has to provision resources selectively for various classes of streams, judiciously sharing the network resources, giving preferential treatment to some service classes.

Traffic oriented: Traffic oriented performance objectives include the aspects that enhance the QOS of traffic streams. In a single class, best effort Internet service model, the key traffic oriented performance objectives include: minimization of packet loss, minimization of delay, maximization of throughput, and enforcement of service level agreements. Under a single class best effort Internet service model, minimization of packet loss is one of the most important traffic oriented performance objectives. Statistically bounded traffic oriented performance objectives (such as peak to peak packet delay variation, loss ratio, and maximum packet transfer delay) might become useful in the forthcoming differentiated services Internet.

Resource oriented: Resource oriented performance objectives include the aspects pertaining to the optimization of resource utilization. Efficient management of network resources is the vehicle for the attainment of resource oriented performance objectives. In particular, it is generally desirable to ensure that subsets of network resources do not become over utilized and congested while other subsets along alternate feasible paths remain underutilized. Bandwidth is a crucial resource in contemporary networks. Therefore, a central function of traffic engineering is to efficiently manage bandwidth resources.

Chapter 2　Transportation System Issue

● Text A　Traffic Problems and Challenges

　　We live in a complex and rapidly developing world . Consequently, at different development stages, the traffic problems have different emphases. However, these problems are challenges to traffic engineering should face up to.

Traffic congestion

　　Nowadays, with the fast development of social economy, the quantity of personal cars is larger and larger. This brings us lots of problems that we must face to. One of the most serious is traffic congestion.

　　Especially if you live in a large and flourishing city, you must have this experience: you have to wait for the traffic moving on again sometimes. Traffic congestion often takes place in arterials or at the rush time. It is more likely to arise in the weekend. The major cities have already taken measures for it. For example, restrict running for odd-numbered and even-numbered days by plate number. Some cities try to restrict purchase to relieve this problem. It's obvious all that can not resolve this problem fundamentally. The government must take effective measures to planning more powerful transportation. It's very hard to achieve in a short time. In the meanwhile it's urgent to resolve.

　　At present, traffic congestion has become a major problem which most city dwellers, especially those who live in metropolis have to confront in their everyday lives.

　　Why is traffic congestion a problem? At first, owing to the fact that the vehicles keep giving off harmful gases during traffic congestion, air pollution and furthermore, global warming will deteriorate. In addition, traffic congestion will affect the effectiveness of work, because the people have to spend much more time on way to office than necessary, and their work will be distracted or delayed. Apart from this, traffic congestion might give rise to more traffic accidents and therefore becomes a menace to people's lives.

　　So harmful traffic congestion is, the number of private cars still goes up rapid. Why? The first reason may be the remoteness of people's workplace. As a result, people have to choose a tool other than walk to go to work. Being flexible and relatively convenient, private car becomes a very attractive choice. Moreover, owning a private car, especially in some developing countries, is itself a symbol of wealth and high social position. In some developed countries, such as USA, it is also the symbol of independence and maturity. Anyway, owning and driving private cars are regarded by many people as basic human rights.

Undoubtedly, traffic congestion must be, and can be alleviated by correct means. In my view, spending more money on public transportation systems may be a feasible means. Needless to say, policies which encourage people to put these systems to full use, for example, giving certain subsidies, are necessary. In the meantime, measures to restrict the use of private cars, such as levying higher taxes on cars or petrol, its fuel, or exerting more restrictions on the distribution of certificate, should be taken.

Traffic congestion exists wherever demand exceeds the capacity of the transportation system. Congestion is most often thought of as a key problem of the urban traffic system, where it is found particularly on major freeways and at intersections on arterial streets. Traffic congestion has a lot of impact to delay, or lost time.

Because it has seemed increasingly impractical to relieve congestion by expanding facilities, intelligent transportation systems (ITS) have been introduced for managing traffic congestion. Some of the technological solutions involve automatic control of individual vehicles, which is claimed to have the potential to reduce time gaps between vehicles in the traffic stream. Other solutions involve improvement to more traditional forms of traffic control, such as improved timing and coordination of urban arterial signal systems or freeway ramp meters. Finally, it is often suggested that traffic congestion can be reduced through better urban land-use planning, or through application of various economic incentives such as congestion pricing (i.e., prices that vary with the level of congestion).

Traffic safety

Traffic safety problems are paid more and more attentions for that it has a direct connection with people's lives and happiness. Traffic accidents are of concern for all modes of transportation, but are perhaps most visible in highways or urban traffic. According to the statistics data provided by the Traffic Management Bureau of the Ministry of Public Security, PRC, the death numbers in the road traffic accidents has shown an incremental trend since 1988. It has exceeded 100,000 persons every year between 2001 and 2004. After taking some effective measures the death numbers of 2008 declines a little comparing with the former years, but still reaches the striking 73,484 persons. The injuries and death numbers caused by the traffic accidents remind us of the traffic safety problem has become one of the primary aspects of our social health problems.

Traffic safety is a continuing challenge for the traffic engineering profession because of public expectations that safety will continue to improve. To some extent this expectation is responsible for the increased legal liability of public agencies for safety problems. One aspect of the challenge will be to meet increasing public expectations for improved safety in the face of increasing public impatience. Another will be to counteract the tendency for accidents to increase with increasing congestion.

Environment protection

One of the most important challenges to the traffic system is that of dealing with its environmental impacts. Based on environmental impact scoping, the large-scale impacts due to the system as a whole include air quality, energy consumption, and land use. The small-scale impacts due to specific transportation facilities and activities include those related to the displacement of residents and businesses due to construction of transportation facilities, noises, impacts on wildlife, impacts on water quality, visual impacts, temporary impacts during construction, and impacts resulting from construction of transportation facilities in environmentally sensitive areas.

For example, highway construction not only changes the natural state of the hydrological structure of water system, but also affects the water quality along the road. So, it is of great importance in the further deep going study of water environmental problem. Generally, the influence of highway construction on water environment can be divided into two phases: the first phase is construction period; the second phase is operating period. For this problem, first of all, the management should be strengthened; secondly, corresponding engineering measures are necessary.

Equality of access

Another traffic issue is how to provide adequate access to the transportation system for all sorts of people. Three groups in particular have been seen as generally underserved. These are the poor, the elderly, and the physically handicapped. Poor people are seen as underserved because they are less likely than other people own automobiles. The elderly and physically handicapped are seen as underserved both because many are unable to operate automobiles and because historically there have been barriers to the use of public transportation by those whose physical mobility is limited.

● Text B Traffic Congestion and Congestion Pricing

For several decades growth of traffic volumes has outstripped investments in road infrastructure. The result has been a relentless increase in traffic congestion. Congestion imposes various costs on travelers: reduced speeds and increased travel times, a decrease in travel time reliability, greater fuel consumption and vehicle wear, inconvenience from rescheduling trips or using alternative travel modes, and (in the longer run) the costs of relocating residences and jobs. The costs of increased travel times and fuel consumption alone are estimated to amount to hundreds of dollars per capita per year in the US (Schrank and Lomax, 1999) and comparable values have been reported for Europe.

Traffic congestion is a consequence of the nature of supply and demand: capacity is time consuming and costly to build and is fixed for long time periods, demand fluctuates over time, and transport services cannot be stored to smooth imbalances between capacity and demand. Various policies to curb traffic congestion have been adopted or proposed over the years. The traditional response is to expand capacity by building new roads or upgrading existing ones. A second method is to reduce demand by discouraging peak-period travel, limiting access to congested areas by using permit systems and parking restrictions, imposing bans on commercial vehicles during certain hours, and so on. A third approach is to improve the efficiency of the road system, so that the same demand can be accommodated at a lower cost. Re-timing of traffic lights, metering access to highway entrance ramps, high-occupancy vehicle lanes and Advanced Traveller Information Systems are examples of such measures.

The topic is concerned with congestion pricing as a tool for alleviating traffic congestion. The insight for congestion pricing comes from the observation that people tend to make socially efficient choices when they are faced with all the social benefits and costs of their actions. As just noted various demand management tools to accomplish this can be used.

But congestion pricing is widely viewed by economists as the most efficient means because it employs the price mechanism, with all its advantages of clarity, universality, and efficiency. Pigou (1920) and Knight (1924) were the first to advocate it. But it was the late William Vickrey, who steadfastly promoted congestion pricing for some forty years, who was arguably the most influential in making the case on both theoretical and practical grounds. In one of his early advocacy pieces, Vickrey (1963) identified the potential for road pricing to influence travellers' choice of route and travel mode, and its implications for land use. He also discussed alternative methods of automated toll collection. Another of his early proposals was to set parking fees in real time as a function of the occupancy rate. An overview of Vickrey's contributions to pricing of urban private and public transport is found in Arnott et al. (1994, pp. 271-5).

As Vickrey's work makes clear, true congestion pricing entails setting tolls that match the severity of congestion, which requires that tolls vary according to time, location, type of vehicle and current circumstances (e.g. accidents or bad weather). Congestion pricing is common in other sectors of the economy — from telephone rates and air fares to hotels and public utilities. But despite the efforts of Vickrey and other economists, congestion pricing is still rarely used on roads. Tolls are not charged on most roads, and fuel taxes do not vary with traffic volumes. And costs of registration, licensing and insurance do not even depend on distance travelled. Nevertheless, the number of applications and experiments in road pricing is slowly growing, spurred on by the combined impetus of worsening traffic conditions and advances in automatic vehicle identification technology. Descriptions of various road pricing schemes, including Singapore's pioneering toll system, Scandinavian toll-rings, and Californian pay-lanes are found in Gómez-Ibáñez and Small (1994) and Small and Gómez-Ibáñez (1998).

There is no explicit treatment of freight transportation. Nothing is said about the implications of congestion pricing for urban structure or the location of new developments. And only passing mention in Section 4 is given to the potential effects of congestion pricing on traffic noise, pollution, and traffic accidents.

Vocabulary and Glossary

1. ban ①*vt.* 禁止,取缔②*n.* 禁令,禁忌
2. curb *n.* ①路缘②勒马绳③抑制;控制;勒住
3. even-numbered *adj.* 偶数的,双数的
4. flourishing ①*adj.* 繁荣的;繁茂的;盛行的②*v.* 茂盛(flourish 的 ing 形式)
5. fluctuate ①*vi.* 波动;涨落;动摇②*vt.* 使波动;使动摇
6. fundamentally *adv.* 根本地,从根本上;基础地
7. heterogeneity *n.* 异质性;不均匀性;多相性
8. hydrological *adj.* 水文学的
9. impetus *n.* 动力;促进;冲力
10. menace ①*n.* 威胁,恐吓②*vi.* 恐吓,进行威胁③*vt.* 威胁,恐吓
11. metropolis *n.* 大都市;首府;重要中心
12. odd-numbered *adj.* 奇数的,单数的
13. peak-period 高峰期
14. stochastic *adj.* 随机的;猜测的
15. Advanced Traveller Information Systems(ATIS)　先进的出行者信息系统
16. automated toll collection　自动收费
17. automatic vehicle identification　车辆自动识别
18. city dwellers　城市居民
19. commercial vehicles　商用车辆
20. congestion pricing　拥挤收费;堵车费;高峰期行车收费
21. construction period　建设期;施工期
22. economic incentive　经济激励;经济刺激
23. energy consumption　能源消耗
24. engineering measures　工程措施
25. entrance ramp　入口坡道;驶入匝道;高速路入口
26. freight transportation　货物运输
27. fuel tax　燃油税
28. high-occupancy vehicle lanes　高占有率车辆专用车道
29. in real time　实时的;及时的;立即
30. operating period　运行期;操作周期
31. parking fees　停车费;泊车费
32. plate number　车牌号码

33. price mechanism 价格机制
34. private car 私家车
35. public transport 公共交通
36. re-timing of traffic lights 交通信号灯的动态调整
37. rush time 高峰期
38. time-independent 不随时间变化的
39. traffic accidents 交通事故
40. traffic congestion 交通拥堵
41. traffic stream 车流

Exercises

I. True or false.

1. Traffic congestion often takes place in the main road or at the rush time. ( )

2. In addition, traffic congestion will affect the effectiveness of work, because people have to spend much less time on way to office than necessary, and their work will be distracted or delayed. ( )

3. Poor people are seen as deserved because they are less likely than other people own automobiles. ( )

4. The injuries and death numbers caused by the traffic accidents remind us that the traffic safety problem has become one of the primary aspects of our social health problems. ( )

5. But congestion pricing is widely viewed by economists as the most efficient way because it employs the price mechanism, with all its advantages of clarity, universality, and efficiency. ( )

II. Choose the best word or phrase to complete each statement.

1. At present, traffic congestion has become a major problem which most city dwellers, especially those who live in _____ have to confront in their everyday lives.
   A. villages   B. metropolis   C. countrysides   D. suburbs

2. _____ is most often thought of as a key problem of the urban traffic system, where it is found particularly on major freeways and at intersections on arterial streets.
   A. Congestion   B. Traffic safety   C. Noise   D. Exhaust gas

3. The elderly and physically _____ are seen as underserved both because many are unable to operate automobiles and because historically there have been barriers to the use of public transportation by those whose physical mobility is limited.
   A. ament   B. defective   C. handicapped   D. properly

4. A second method is to reduce demand by discouraging _____ travel, limiting access to congested areas by using permit systems and parking restrictions, imposing bans on commercial ve-

hicles during certain hours, and so on.

    A. slack hours   B. peak-period   C. low cycle   D. normal time range

5. The insight for congestion pricing comes from the observation that people tend to make socially _____ choices when they are faced with all the social benefits and costs of their actions.

    A. efficiency   B. effictive   C. productivity   D. efficient

III. Translate the following sentences into Chinese.

1. At first, owing to the fact that the vehicles keep giving off harmful gases during traffic congestion, air pollution and furthermore, global warming will deteriorate.

2. In the meantime, measures to restrict the use of private cars, such as levying higher taxes on cars or petrol, its fuel, or exerting more restrictions on the distribution of certificate, should be taken.

3. For example, highway construction not only changes the natural state of the hydrological structure of water system, but also affects the water quality along the road.

4. The elderly and physically handicapped are seen as underserved both because many are unable to operate automobiles and because historically there have been barriers to the use of public transportation by those whose physical mobility is limited.

5. Congestion imposes various costs on travellers: reduced speeds and increased travel times, a decrease in travel time reliability, greater fuel consumption and vehicle wear, inconvenience from rescheduling trips or using alternative travel modes, and (in the longer run) the costs of relocating residences and jobs.

IV. Discussions.

1. What is the cause of traffic congestion? Why is traffic congestion a problem?

2. Various policies to curb traffic congestion have been adopted or proposed over the years, please give the details.

Reading Material: Ten-day Chinese Traffic Jam

Motorists in China are experiencing a traffic jam from the hell. Thousands of drivers have been stuck in their cars for ten days on the Beijing-Tibet Expressway just outside the Chinese capital. The gridlock started on August 14th when roadworks began. The bad news is that the chaos will continue for another month. The tailbacks stretch back for 100km. The situation has been made worse by dozens of cars breaking down or overheating. Around 400 traffic polices have been assigned to patrol the jam to make sure tensions don't rise too far. The horrendous snarl-up is the result of the explosion in the number of cars on Chinese roads. As China becomes wealthier, more people are buying cars, thus causing more traffic problems.

Drivers trapped in the traffic jam know they have to be patient and sit for long hours in their cars. There are no showers for them to use and if they need to use a toilet, they have to lock their cars and wander off to the nearest café. There are many complaints of local people taking advantage of the stranded motorists by charging them more than double prices for drinks and snacks. People are keeping themselves busy by playing cards or board games. Some have reported feeling homesick. One truck driver Juang Shao expressed his frustration over the situation: "I've missed my daughter's birthday and the food in my truck has probably turned into soup," he said. He said he was worried his truck would be stuck in the traffic forever.

Can China Avoid Getting Stuck in Traffic?

Amid a frenzy of car buying, the Chinese are losing the race for traffic space, but it's not too late for them to take another road.

Transportation experts say there's barely enough space on the roads in China's largest cities for the 35 million cars that were bought during the past decade of frenzied consumerism. (Remko Tanis/Flickr.com)

The new Great Wall of China is the "Great Wall" of cars stuck in city traffic, researchers say, and it will take more than restrictions on new license plates and car registrations to break the gridlock.

The problem is, there's barely enough space on the roads in China's largest cities for the 35 million cars that were bought during the past decade of frenzied consumerism, according to transportation experts at the University of California, Berkeley, and Massachusetts Institute of Technology.

In the ancient capital city of Xi'an, home of the buried armies of terracotta warriors, Lee Schipper said the joke that if you want to drive in through the North Gate, you should call your friend who's leaving through the South Gate, so you can arrange to take his place. Schipper is a senior project scientist at UC Berkeley's Global Metro Studies Center and a co-author of a 2010 study on China's crowded cities.

"The number of cars is going up much faster in China than the length of the roads in the cities," Schipper said, "The greatest 'communist' society ever invented doesn't know what to do. That's what worries me. Cars are not something any kind of government can easily control if they're cheap to buy and cheap to drive."

In Shanghai, a city of more than 20 million where new car registrations are restricted to 6,000 monthly, commuter traffic has slowed to 6 to 10 miles per hour, well under the speed of a bicycle. The traffic's a mess, even though only 20 percent of all daily trips in Shanghai are by car, compared to 80 percent in U.S. cities. For the majority of Shanghaians, who are walking or biking or waiting at the bus stops, it means breathing in a lot of bad air.

"It's what I call hyper-motorization," Schipper said. "China's cities have expanded to make room for cars, but congestion levels have spiraled upward and average speeds downward. Things freeze up regularly."

Building more roads and adding lanes, as China is doing, will not solve the problem, Schipper said. The amount of urbanized land in Beijing has tripled since 1990, but now commutes are longer. China could build more cities, but the new roads would fill up quickly, too.

Schipper and co-authors Wei-Shiuen Ng and Yang Chen, Ph. D. students at UC Berkeley and MIT, respectively, suggest that China has a window of opportunity to solve its traffic woes before car ownership jumps much higher. If China were to hike its fuel tax on gasoline, levy tolls at rush hour, raise parking fees, encourage compact development along bus lines, and give up more road space to cyclists and fast bus routes, it could get the traffic moving and avoid potentially much worse gridlock, the researchers found.

"Every motorist should know what it really costs to bring a car into a zone where land space is scarce," Schipper said.

Most people in China still travel by bus, bike or on foot. There are only 18 private vehicles for every 1,000 Chinese—roughly the level of ownership back in the 1920s in the United States. Today, there are 740 private vehicles for every 1,000 Americans. The average resident of China travels only 600 miles per year by bus, train, car or plane, compared to 15,000 motorized miles per capita for Americans.

But China is now the top auto market in the world, having surpassed the U. S. in sales in 2009. Last year, General Motors Co. sold more cars in China than in the U. S. If current trends continue, the research shows, China can expect 146 million private cars by 2020, or four times the number it has now.

"My role is not telling China what to do," said Schipper, who has traveled to the country 20 times in the past decade to talk to city and transportation planners. "I can point to the consequences of what they do. The present path in China is towards more and more cars. Smaller towns of under 2 million people are not as crowded, but then people flee to the smaller towns and they get gummed up, too."

This month, Beijing officials launched a lottery for new license plates to restrict new cars in the city to 240,000 in 2011. Last year, more than 700,000 cars were sold in the city. But the measure may backfire, Schipper said. Beijing residents rushed to buy 20,000 cars the day before the lottery went into effect; and people will likely drive their cars more now, sharing them with family and friends. Events such as the 10-day, 60-mile traffic jam on the outskirts of Beijing last summer could become more common.

A number of Chinese cities, including Beijing, are building rapid transit systems in which buses can travel in segregated lanes with priority at intersections. But these efforts to boost mass transportation are being overwhelmed.

"The Chinese don't have much time," Schipper said. "The longer they wait or take missteps, the harder it will be to recover. More and more consumers will be used to owning and using cars, and city development will be distorted increasingly towards a car-oriented pattern. The experience from nearby cities in Asia — Bangkok, Jakarta and Manila, to give three notorious examples — suggest that recovering from this pattern will be very, very difficult."

Part II

专业篇

Chapter 3 Traffic Flow

◆ Text A Traffic Flow Parameters

At any given time, there are millions of vehicles on our roadways. These vehicles interact with each other and impact the overall movement of traffic, or the traffic flow. Whether the task is evaluating the capacity of existing roadways or designing new roadways, most transportation engineering projects begin with an evaluation of the traffic flow. Therefore, the transportation engineer needs to have a firm understanding of the theories behind traffic flow analysis.

Traffic flow can be divided into two primary types. Understanding what type of flow is occurring in a given situation will help you decide which analysis methods and descriptions are the most relevant. The first type is called uninterrupted flow, and is flow regulated by vehicle-vehicle interactions and interactions between vehicles and the roadway. For example, vehicles traveling on an interstate highway are participating in uninterrupted flow. The second type of traffic flow is called interrupted flow. Interrupted flow is flow regulated by an external means, such as a traffic signal. Under interrupted flow conditions, vehicle-vehicle interactions and vehicle-roadway interactions play a secondary role in defining the traffic flow.

Traffic Flow Parameters

Traffic flow is a difficult phenomenon to describe without the use of a common set of terms. The following paragraphs will introduce most of the common terms that are used in discussions about traffic flow.

Speed (v)

The speed of a vehicle is defined as the distance it travels per unit of time. Most of the time, each vehicle on the roadway will have a speed that is somewhat different from those around it. In quantifying the traffic flow, the average speed of the traffic is the significant variable. The average speed, called the space mean speed, can be found by averaging the individual speeds of all of the vehicles in the study area.

Volume

Volume is simply the number of vehicles that pass a given point on the roadway in a specified period of time. By counting the number of vehicles that pass a point on the roadway during a 15-minute period, you can arrive at the 15-minute volume. Volume is commonly converted directly to flow (q), which is a more useful parameter.

Flow (q)

Flow is one of the most common traffic parameters. Flow is the rate at which vehicles pass a given point on the roadway, and is normally given in terms of vehicles per hour. The 15-minute volume can be converted to a flow by multiplying the volume by four. If 15-minute volume was 100 cars, we would report the flow as 400 vehicles per hour. For that 15-minute interval of time, vehicles were crossing the designated point at a rate of 400 vehicles/hour.

Peak Hour Factor (PHF)

The ratio of the hourly flow rate (q_{60}) divided by the peak 15 minute rate of flow expressed as an hourly flow (q_{15}).

$$\text{PHF} = \frac{q_{60}}{q_{15}}$$

Density (k)

Density refers to the number of vehicles present on a given length of roadway. Normally, density is reported in terms of vehicles per mile or vehicles per kilometer. High densities indicate that individual vehicles are very close together, while low densities imply greater distances between vehicles.

Headway, spacing, gap, and clearance are all various measures for describing the space between vehicles. These parameters are discussed in the paragraphs below.

Headway (h)

Headway is a measure of the temporal space between two vehicles. Specifically, the headway is the time that elapses between the arrival of the leading vehicle and the following vehicle at the designated test point. You can measure the headway between two vehicles by starting a chronograph when the front bumper of the first vehicle crosses the selected point, and subsequently recording the time that the second vehicle's front bumper crosses over the designated point. Headway is usually reported in units of seconds.

Spacing (s)

Spacing is the physical distance, usually reported in feet or meters, between the front bumper of the leading vehicle and the front bumper of the following vehicle. Spacing complements headway, as it describes the same space in another way. Spacing is the product of speed and headway.

Gap (g)

Gap is very similar to headway, except that it is a measure of the time that elapses between the departure of the first vehicle and the arrival of the second at the designated test point. Gap is a measure of the time between the rear bumper of the first vehicle and the front bumper of the second vehicle, where headway focuses on front-to-front times. Gap is usually reported in units of seconds.

Clearance (c)

Clearance is similar to spacing, except that the clearance is the distance between the rear bumper of the leading vehicle and the front bumper of the following vehicle. The clearance is equivalent to the spacing minus the length of the leading vehicle. Clearance, like spacing, is usually reported in units of feet or meters.

➡ Text B Traffic Flow Theory

Speed-Flow-Density Relationship

Speed, flow, and density are all related to each other. The relationships between speed and density are not difficult to observe in the real world, while the effects of speed and density on flow are not quite as apparent.

Under uninterrupted flow conditions, speed, density, and flow are all related by the following equation:

$$q = k \times v$$

Where: q = Flow (vehicles/hour);

k = Density (vehicles/mile, vehicles/kilometer);

v = Speed (miles/hour, kilometers/hour).

Because flow is the product of speed and density, the flow is equal to zero when one or both of these terms is zero. It is also possible to deduce that the flow is maximized at some critical combination of speed and density.

Two common traffic conditions illustrate these points. The first is the modern traffic jam, where traffic densities are very high and speeds are very low. This combination produces a very low flow. The second condition occurs when traffic densities are very low and drivers can obtain free flow speed without any undue stress caused by other vehicles on the roadway. The extremely low density compensates for the high speeds, and the resulting flow is very low.

Special Speed & Density Conditions

The discussion of the speed-flow-density relationship mentioned several speed-density conditions. Two of these conditions are extremely significant and have been given special names.

Free Flow Speed

This is the mean speed that vehicles will travel on a roadway when the density of vehicles is low. Under low-density conditions, drivers no longer worry about other vehicles. They subsequently proceed at speeds that are controlled by the performance of their vehicles, the conditions of the roadway, and the posted speed limit.

Jam Density

Extremely high densities can bring traffic on a roadway to a complete stop. The density at which traffic stops is called the jam density.

Greenshield's Model

Greenshield was able to develop a model of uninterrupted traffic flow that predicts and explains the trends that are observed in real traffic flows. While Greenshield's model is not perfect, it is fairly accurate and relatively simple.

Greenshield made the assumption that, under uninterrupted flow conditions, speed and density are linearly related. This relationship is expressed mathematically and graphically below. See Figure 3.1.

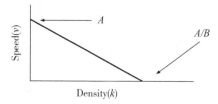

Figure 3.1 Speed vs. Density

$$v = A - B \times k$$

Where: v = speed (miles/hour, kilometers/hour);
A, B = constants determined from field observations;
k = density (vehicles/mile, vehicles/kilometer).

As noted above, you can determine the values of the constants A and B through field observations. This is normally done by collecting velocity and density data in the field, plotting the data, and then using linear regression to fit a line through the data points. The constant A represents the free flow speed, while A/B represents the jam density.

Inserting Greenshield's speed-density relationship into the general speed-flow-density relationship yields the following equations:

$$q = (A - B \times k) \times k$$

or

$$q = A \times k - B \times k^2$$

Where: q = flow (vehicles/hour);
A, B = constants;
k = density (vehicles/mile, vehicles/kilometer).

This new relationship between flow and density (Figure 3.2) provides an avenue for finding the density at which the flow is maximized.

$$\frac{dq}{dk} = A - 2 \times B \times k$$

setting $dq/dK = 0$ yields:

$$k = \frac{A}{2 \times B}$$

Therefore, at the density given above, the flow will be maximized. Substituting this maximized value of k into the original speed-density relationship yields the speed at which the flow is maximized.

$$v = A - B \times \frac{A}{2 \times B} \quad \text{or} \quad v = \frac{A}{2}$$

This indicates that the maximum flow occurs when traffic is flowing at half of free-flow speed (A). Substituting the optimum speed and density into the speed-flow-density relationship yields the maximum flow.

$$q = \frac{A}{2} \times \frac{A}{2 \times B} \quad \text{or} \quad q = \frac{A^2}{4 \times B}$$

Figure 3.3 shows the relationship between flow and speed graphically.

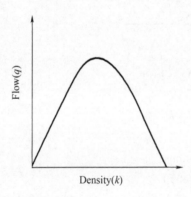
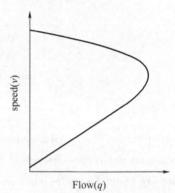

Figure 3.2 Flow vs. Density   Figure 3.3 Flow vs. Speed

As you can see, Greenshield's model is quite powerful.

The following can be derived from Greenshield's model:

- When the density is zero, the flow is zero because there are no vehicles on the roadway.
- As the density increases, the flow also increases to some maximum flow conditions.
- When the density reaches a maximum, generally called jam density, the flow must be zero because the vehicles tend to line up end to end (parking lot conditions).

As the density increases the flow increases to some maximum value, but a continual increase in density will cause the flow to decrease until jam density and zero flow conditions are reached.

Time-Space Diagrams

A time-space diagram is commonly used to solve a number of transportation- related problems. Typically, time is drawn on the horizontal axis and distance from a reference point on the vertical axis. The trajectories of individual vehicles in motion are portrayed in this diagram by sloping lines, and stationary vehicles are represented by horizontal lines. The slope of the line represents the speed of the vehicle. Curved portions of the trajectories represent vehicles undergoing speed changes such as deceleration.

Diagrams that show the position of individual vehicles in time and in space are very useful for understanding traffic flow. These diagrams are especially useful for discussions of shock waves and wave propagation.

The time-space diagram is a graph that describes the relationship between the location of vehicles in a traffic stream and the time as the vehicles progress along the highway. The following diagram(Figure 3.4) is an example of a time-space diagram.

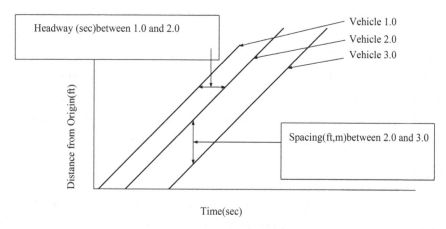

Figure 3.4   Example of a Time-Space Diagram

Time-space diagrams are created by plotting the position of each vehicle, given as a distance from a reference point, against time. The first vehicle will probably start at the origin, while the vehicles that follow won't reach the reference point until slightly later times. Reductions in speed cause the slopes of the lines to flatten, while increases in speed cause the slopes to become greater. Acceleration causes the time-space curve for the accelerating vehicle to bend until the new speed is attained. Curves that cross indicate that the vehicles both shared the same position at the same time. Unless passing is permitted, crossed curves indicate collisions.

Shock Waves

Shock waves that occur in traffic flow are very similar to the waves produced by dropping stones in water. A shock wave propagates along a line of vehicles in response to changing conditions at the front of the line. Shock waves can be generated by collisions, sudden increases in speed caused by entering free flow conditions, or by a number of other means. Basically, a shock wave exists whenever the traffic conditions change.

The equation that is used to estimate the propagation velocity of shock waves is given below.

$$v_{sw} = \frac{q_b - q_a}{k_b - k_a}$$

Where: v_{sw} = propagation velocity of shock wave (miles/hour);

q_b = flow prior to change in conditions (vehicles/hour);

q_a = flow after change in conditions (vehicles/hour);

k_b = traffic density prior to change in conditions (vehicles/mile);

k_a = traffic density after change in conditions (vehicles/mile).

Note the magnitude and direction of the shock wave.

(+) Shock wave is travelling in same direction as traffic stream.

(−) Shock wave is traveling upstream or against the traffic stream.

For example, let's assume that an accident has occurred and that the flow after the accident is reduced to zero. Initially, the flow was several vehicles per hour. Also, the density is much greater after the accident. Substituting these values into the shock wave equation yields a negative (−) propagation velocity. This means that the shock wave is traveling against the traffic. If you could look down on this accident, you would see a wave front, at which vehicles began to slow from their initial speed, passing from vehicle to vehicle back up the traffic stream. The first car would notice the accident first, followed an instant later by the second car. Each vehicle begins slowing after its driver recognizes that the preceding vehicle is slowing.

Queuing Theory

Greenshield's model was developed to aid our understanding of uninterrupted flow. Unfortunately, Greenshield's model is unable to cope with the added complexities that are generated under interrupted flow conditions. Interrupted flow requires an understanding of Queuing Theory, which is an entirely separate model of traffic flow.

Queuing Theory can be used to analyze the flow of traffic on the approach to and through an intersection controlled by a traffic signal. This is accomplished by analyzing the cumulative passage of vehicles as a function of time. The queuing diagram for interrupted flow shows the flow on one intersection approach. Traffic is stopped from time t_1 to t_2 during the red signal interval. At the start of the green interval (t_2), traffic begins to leave the intersection at the saturation flow rate (q_G), and continues until the queue is exhausted. Thereafter, the departure rate $D(t)$, equals the arrival rate, $A(t)$, until t_3 which is the beginning of the next red signal. At this point, the process starts over.

Vocabulary and Glossary

1. convert *v.* (使)转变
2. designate *v.* 指明,指出;指派;表明,意味着
3. density *n.* 密度,车流密度

4. external *adj.* 外面的,外部的;表面上的;外用的

5. flow *n.* 交通(流)量

6. gap *n.* 车辆时距,指同一车流中前车尾部与后车前部的车辆时间距离

7. headway *n.* 车头时距,指同一车流中前车头(尾)部与后车头(尾)部的车辆时间距离

8. insert *v.* 插入;嵌入;(在文章中)添加;加插

9. interrupted flow 间断流

10. regress *v.* 回归;退回

11. relevant *adj.* 有关的,相关联的;实质性的

12. shockwaves *n.* 车流波(常见于瓶颈路段);车流波速等于车流量的变化与车流密度变化的比值

13. spacing *n.* 车头间距

14. Jam Density 阻塞密度

15. PHF (Peak Hour Factor) 高峰小时系数

16. space mean speed 空间平均速度

17. time mean speed 时间平均速度

18. travel time 行程时间

19. uninterrupted flow 连续流

Exercises

I. True or false.

1. Traffic flow can be divided into two primary types which are uninterrupted flow and interrupted flow. ( )

2. Spacing complements headway, as it describes the same space in another way. Spacing is the product of speed and headway. ( )

3. When traffic densities are very low and drivers can obtain free flow speed without any undue stress caused by other vehicles on the roadway, the resulting flow is very high. ( )

4. In Greenshield's mode ($v = A - B \times k$), the constant A represents the free flow speed, while B represents the jam density. ( )

5. In Greenshield's mode, when the density reaches a maximum, generally called jam density, the flow must be zero because the vehicles tend to line up end to end. ( )

II. Choose the best word or phrase to complete each statement.

1. The average speed, called the space mean speed, can be found by _____ the individual speeds of all of the vehicles in the study area.

A. adding B. averaging C. multiplying D. dividing

2. Flow is the _____ at which vehicles pass a given point on the roadway, and is normally

given in terms of vehicles per hour.

    A. quantity   B. number   C. amount   D. rate

3. The _____ is the time that elapses between the arrival of the leading vehicle and the following vehicle at the designated test point.

    A. gap   B. headway   C. spacing   D. clearance

4. In a time-space diagram, the _____ of the line represents the speed of the vehicle.

    A. slope   B. length   C. width   D. height

5. Time-space diagrams are created by plotting the position of each vehicle, given as a _____ from a reference point.

    A. time   B. space   C. length   D. distance

III. Translate the following sentences into Chinese.

1. Under interrupted flow conditions, vehicle-vehicle interactions and vehicle-roadway interactions play a secondary role in defining the traffic flow.

2. High densities indicate that individual vehicles are very close together, while low densities imply greater distances between vehicles.

3. Gap is a measure of the time between the rear bumper of the first vehicle and the front bumper of the second vehicle, where headway focuses on front-to-front times.

4. This is normally done by collecting velocity and density data in the field, plotting the data, and then using linear regression to fit a line through the data points.

5. The trajectories of individual vehicles in motion are portrayed in this diagram by sloping lines, and stationary vehicles are represented by horizontal lines.

IV. Discussions.

1. What will generate shock waves?

2. According to text B, explain the Queuing Theory in your own words.

Reading Material: Travel Time Studies

Travel time studies are often used specifically to evaluate the extent and causes of congestion. Travel time studies generally involve significant lengths of a facility, or group of facilities. Information on travel time between key points within the study sections is sought, and is used to identify those sections or segments in need of improvement. Such studies are normally coordinated with delay observations, and stopped delay is the most easily observed measure.

Travel time information is used for many purposes:

- to identify problem locations on facilities by virtue of high travel times and delays;
- to measure arterial level of service, based on average travel speeds and travel times;
- to provide necessary input to traffic assignment model, which focus on linktravel times as a

key determinant of the route selected by the driver;
- to provide travel time data for economic evaluations of transportation improvements, in which the economic value of travel time is a major factor;
- to develop contour maps and other depictions of traffic congestion in an area or region.

Field Techniques

Because travel time studies take place over an extended length of a facility, the most frequently-used methodology for collecting data is by running test cars through the section and making observations of intermediate travel times and stopped delays at key locations along the study route.

To assure some uniformity of data, drivers of test vehicles are instructed to use one of three driving strategies:

Floating Car Technique: In this procedure, the driver of the test car is instructed to pass as many vehicles as pass the test car. In this way, the average position of the vehicle in the traffic stream is maintained, and measurements tend to reflect average conditions within the traffic stream. Such a driving technique is productive when volumes are low, or when there is a single lane in each direction of travel. On a freeway, however, this could become very difficult, as passings occur frequently, and congestion may prevent a test-car driver from maintaining his/her position safely.

Maximum Car Technique: In this procedure, the driver is instructed to drive as fast as is safely practical in the traffic stream, without ever driving faster than the design speed of the facility. This is a less stressful procedure, but does not tend to estimate average conditions within the traffic stream. When using this technique, travel times reflect the faster range of the traffic stream, and often approximate 85th percentile average travel speeds.

Average Car Technique: In this procedure, the driver is asked to approximate the average conditions in the traffic stream, using his/her judgment only. This is a less stressful driving approach, but leaves a great deal to the judgment of individual drivers. Consistency of data may be somewhat compromised here, although the method will approximate average conditions in the traffic stream.

Issues related to sample size are handled similarly to spot speed studies. One of the reasons for specifying a driving strategy for test cars is to restrict the standard deviation of test-car results—leading to smaller required sample sizes. For most common applications, the required number of test-car runs ranges between 6 and 10 at the low end, to approximately 50 at the high end. The latter number is difficult to achieve without affecting traffic, and may require that runs be taken over an extended period of time, such as the evening rush hour over several days.

Chapter 4 Traffic Control

● Text A Introduction to Traffic Control

Traffic Congestion and the Need for Traffic Control

Transportation has always been a crucial aspect of human civilization, but it is only in the second half of the last century that the phenomenon of traffic congestion has become predominant due to the rapid increase in the number of vehicles and in the transportation demand in virtually all transportation modes. Traffic congestion appears when too many vehicles attempt to use a common transportation infrastructure with limited capacity. In the best case, traffic congestion leads to queuing phenomena (and corresponding delays) while the infrastructure capacity ("the server") is fully utilized. In the worst (and far more typical) case, traffic congestion leads to a degraded use of the available infrastructure (reduced throughput), thus contributing to an accelerated congestion increase, which leads to further infrastructure degradation, and so forth. Traffic congestion results in excess delays, reduced safety, and increased environmental pollution. The following impressive statement is included in the European Commission's "White Paper—European Transport Policy for 2010": "Because of congestion, there is a serious risk that Europe will lose economic competitiveness. The most recent study on the subject showed that the external costs of road traffic congestion alone amount to 0.5% of Community GDP.

Traffic forecasts for the next 10 years show that if nothing is done, road congestion will increase significantly by 2010. The costs attributable to congestion will also increase by 142% to reach 80 billion a year, which is approximately 1% of Community GDP." The emergence of traffic (i.e., many interacting vehicles using a common infrastructure) and subsequently traffic congestion (whereby demand temporarily exceeds the infrastructure capacity) have opened new innovation needs in the transportation area. The energy crisis in the 1970s, the increased importance of environmental concerns, and the limited economic and physical resources are among the most important reasons why a brute force approach (i.e., the continuous expansion of the available transportation infrastructure) cannot continue to be the only answer to the ever increasing transportation and mobility needs of modern societies. The efficient, safe, and less polluting transportation of persons and goods calls for an optimal utilization of the available infrastructure via suitable application of a variety of traffic control measures. This trend is enabled by the rapid developments in the areas of communications and computing (telematics), but it is quite evident that the efficiency of traffic control directly depends on the efficiency and relevance of the employed control methodologies. This paper provides an overview of advanced traffic control strategies for three particular areas: urban road networks, freeway networks, and route guidance and information systems.

Introduction to Traffic Control Devices

Traffic control devices are the media by which traffic engineers communicate with drivers. Virtually every traffic law, regulation, or operating instruction must be communicated through the use of devices that fall into three broad categories: traffic markings, traffic signs and traffic signals.

Traffic Markings

Traffic markings serve a variety of purposes and functions and fall into three broad categories: longitudinal markings, transverse markings, object markers and delineators.

- Longitudinal markings are those markings placed parallel to the direction of travel. Which provide guidance for the placement of vehicles on the traveled way cross-section and basic trajectory guidance for vehicles traveling along the facilities. The vast majority of longitudinal markings involve centerlines, lane lines, and pavement edge lines.

- Transverse markings include any and all markings with a component that cuts across a portion or all of the traveled way. Which involve stop lines, crosswalk markings, parking space markings, word and symbol markings etc. When used, all transverse markings are white.

- Object markers are used to denote obstructions either in or adjacent to the traveled way. Delineators are reflective devices mounted at a 4-ft height on the side(s) of a roadway to help denote its alignment. They are particularly useful during inclement weather, where pavement edge markings may not be visible.

Traffic Signs

In general, traffic signs fall into one of three major categories:

- Regulatory signs. Which convey information concerning specific traffic regulations. Regulations may relate to right-of-way, speed limits, lane usage, parking, or a variety of other functions.

- Warning signs. Which are used to inform drivers about upcoming hazards that they might not see or otherwise discern in time to safely react.

- Guide signs. Which provide information on routes, destinations, and services that drivers may be seeking.

Traffic Signals

The MUTCD defines nine types of traffic signals:

- Traffic control signals;
- Pedestrian signals;
- Emergency vehicle traffic control signals;
- Traffic control signals for one-lane, two-way facilities;
- Traffic control signals for freeway entrance ramps;
- Traffic control signals for moveable bridges;
- Lane-use control signals;
- Flashing beacons;
- In-roadway lights.

The most common of these is the traffic control signal, used at busy intersections to direct traffic to alternately stop and move.

Text B Road Traffic Control

Basic Notions

Traffic lights at intersections are the major control measures in urban road networks. Traffic lights were originally installed in order to guarantee the safe crossing of antagonistic streams of vehicles and pedestrians; with steadily increasing traffic demands, it was soon realized that, once traffic lights exist, they may lead (under equally safe traffic conditions) to more or less efficient network operations, hence there must exist an optimal control strategy leading to minimization of the total time spent by all vehicles in the network. Although the corresponding optimal control problem may be readily formulated for any road network, its real-time solution and realization in a control loop faces a number of apparently insurmountable difficulties.

- The red-green switchings of traffic lights call for the introduction of discrete variables, which renders the optimization problem combinatorial.
- The size of the problem for a whole network is very large.
- Many unpredictable and hardly measurable disturbances (incidents, illegal parking, pedestrian crossings, intersection blocking, etc.) may perturb the traffic flow.
- Measurements of traffic conditions are mostly local (via inductive loop detectors) and highly noisy due to various effects.
- There are tight real-time constraints, e.g., decision making within 2s for advanced control systems.

The combination of these difficulties renders the solution of a detailed optimal control problem infeasible for more than one intersection. Therefore, proposed control strategies for road traffic control introduce a number of simplifications of different kinds or address only a part of the related traffic control problems. Unfortunately, most proposed simplifications render the corresponding control strategies less suitable to address traffic saturation phenomena.

An intersection consists of a number of approaches and the crossing area. An approach may have one or more lanes but has a unique, independent queue. Approaches are used by corresponding traffic streams (veh/h). A saturation flow is the average flow crossing the stop line of an approach when the corresponding stream has right of way (r. o. w.), the upstream demand (or the waiting queue) is sufficiently large, and the downstream links are not blocked by queues. Two compatible streams can safely cross the intersection simultaneously, else they are called antagonistic.

A signal cycle is one repetition of the basic series of signal combinations at an intersection; its duration is called cycle time. A stage (or phase) is a part of the signal cycle, during which one set of streams has r. o. w. (Figure 4.1). Constant lost (or intergreen) times of a few seconds are necessary between stages to avoid interference between antagonistic streams of consecutive stages (Figure 4.2).

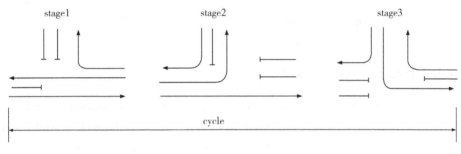

Figure 4.1   Example of signal cycle

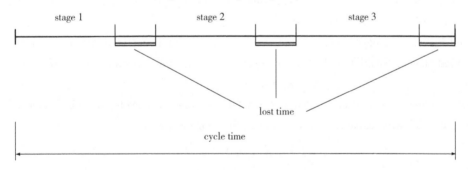

Figure 4.2   Cycle time and lost times

There are four possibilities for influencing traffic conditions via traffic lights operation.

- Stage specification: For complex intersections involving a large number of streams, the specification of the optimal number and constitution of stages is a nontrivial task that can have a major impact on intersection capacity and efficiency.
- Split: This is the relative green duration of each stage (as a portion of the cycle time) that should be optimized according to the demand of the involved streams.
- Cycle time: Longer cycle times typically increase the intersection capacity because the proportion of the constant lost times becomes accordingly smaller; on the other hand, longer cycle times may increase vehicle delays in undersaturated intersections due to longer waiting times during the red phase.

● Offset: This is the phase difference between cycles for successive intersections that may give rise to a "green wave" along an arterial; clearly, the specification of offset should ideally take into account the possible existence of vehicle queues. Control strategies employed for road traffic control may be classified according to the following characteristics.

● Fixed-time strategies for a given time of day (e.g., morning peak hour) are derived off-line by use of appropriate optimization codes based on historical constant demands and turning rates for each stream; traffic-responsive strategies make use of real-time measurements (typically one or two inductive loops per link) to calculate in real time the suitable signal settings.

● Isolated strategies are applicable to single intersections while coordinated strategies consider an urban zone or even a whole network comprising many intersections.

● Most available strategies are only applicable to undersaturated traffic conditions, whereby vehicle queues are only created during the red phases and are dissolved during the green phases; very few strategies are suitable also for oversaturated conditions with partially increasing queues that in many cases reach the upstream intersections.

Isolated Intersection Control

Fixed-Time Strategies: Isolated fixed-time strategies are only applicable to undersaturated traffic conditions. Stage-based strategies under this class determine the optimal splits and cycle time so as to minimize the total delay or maximize the intersection capacity. Phase-based strategies determine not only optimal splits and cycle time but also the optimal staging, which may be an important feature for complex intersections.

Well-known examples of stage-based strategies are SIGSET and SIGCAP proposed. Assuming prespecified stages, SIGSET and SIGCAP specify the splits and the cycle time. Note that

$$\lambda_0 + \lambda_1 + \cdots + \lambda_m = 1 \qquad (4.1)$$

holds by definition, where , and is the total lost time in a cycle. In order to avoid queue building, the following capacity constraint must hold for each stream:

$$s_j \sum_{i=1}^{m} \alpha_{ij} \lambda_i \geq d_j \qquad \forall j \qquad (4.2)$$

Where(4.1) and(4.2) are the saturation flow and the demand, respectively, of stream ; is one if stream has r. o. w. at stage , and zero else. Inequality (4.1) requires that the demand of stream should not be higher than the maximum possible flow assigned to this stream. Finally, a maximum-cycle and minimum-green constraints are also taken into account.

A nonlinear total delay function derived by Webster for undersaturated conditions is used in SIGSET as an optimization objective. Thus, SIGSET solves a linearly constrained nonlinear programming problem to minimize the total intersection delay for given stream demands. On the other hand, SIGCAP may be used to maximize the intersection's capacity as follows. Assume that the real demand is not as in (4.1) but with . SIGCAP replaces in (4.1) by and maximizes under the same constraints as SIGSET, which leads to a linear programming problem. Note that, for reasons mentioned earlier, capacity maximization always leads to the maximum allowable cycle time.

Clearly, SIGCAP should be used for intersections with high demand variability in order to prevent oversaturation, while SIGSET may be used under sufficient capacity margins by replacing in (4.1) by, where are prespecified margin parameters. Phase-based approaches solve a similar problem, suitably extended to consider different staging combinations.

Phase-based approaches consider the compatibility relations of involved streams as prespecified and deliver the optimal staging, splits, and cycle time, so as to minimize total delay or maximize the intersection capacity. The resulting optimization problem is of the binary-mixed-integer-linear-programming type, which calls for branch-and-bound methods for an exact solution. The related computation time is naturally much higher than for stage-based approaches, but this is of minor importance, as calculations are performed offline.

Traffic-Responsive Strategies: Isolated, traffic-responsive strategies make use of real-time measurements provided by inductive loop detectors that are usually located some 40 m upstream of the stop line, to execute some more or less sophisticated vehicle-actuation logic. One of the simplest strategies under this class is the vehicle-interval *method* that is applicable to two-stage intersections. Minimum-green durations are assigned to both stages. If no vehicle passes the related detectors during the minimum green of a stage, the strategy proceeds to the next stage. If a vehicle is detected, a critical interval (CI) is created, during which any detected vehicle leads to a green prolongation that allows the vehicle to cross the intersection. If no vehicle is detected during CI, the strategy proceeds to the next stage, else a new CI is created, and so forth, until a prespecified maximum-green value is reached. An extension of the method also considers the traffic demand on the antagonistic approaches to decide whether to proceed to the next stage or not.

A more sophisticated version of this kind of strategies was proposed by Miller and is included in the control tool MOVA. Miller's strategy answers every seconds the question: Should the switching to the next stage take place now, or should this decision be postponed by T?

To answer this question, the strategy calculates (under certain simplifying assumptions) the time gains and losses caused in all approaches if the decision is postponed by seconds. The corresponding net time gains are combined in a single criterion, and if, the switching takes place immediately, else the decision is postponed until the next time step. A comparative field evaluation of these simple algorithms is presented in.

Fixed-Time Coordinated Control

The most popular representatives of this class of strategies for urban networks are outlined below. By their natures, fixed-time strategies are only applicable to undersaturated traffic conditions.

MAXBAND: The first version of MAXBAND was developed by Little. MAXBAND considers a two-way arterial with n signals (intersections) and specifies the corresponding offsets so as to maximize the number of vehicles that can travel within a given speed range without stopping at any signal (green wave); see Figure. 4.3.

Splits are considered in MAXBAND as given (in accordance with the lateral street demands); hence, the problem consists in placing the known red durations (see the horizontal lines of each signal in Figure 4.3) of the arterial's signals so as to maximize the inbound and outbound bandwidths respectively.

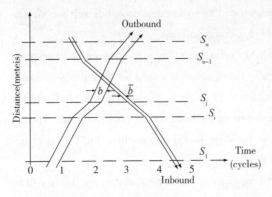

Figure 4.3 A maximum band along an arterial

For an appropriate problem formulation, it is necessary to introduce some binary decision variables, which leads to a binary-mixed-integer-linear-programming problem. The employed branch-and-bound solution method benefits from a number of nice properties of this particular problem to reduce the required computational effort. Attempts to farther reduce the computational efforts required by the method are reported. Little extended the basic MAXBAND method via incorporation of some cycle constraints to render it applicable also to networks of arterials. MAXBAND has been applied to several road networks in North America and beyond. A number of significant extensions have been introduced in the original method in order to consider a variety of new aspects such as: time of clearance of existing queue, left-turn movements, and different bandwidths for each link of the arterial (MULTIBAND).

TRANSYT: TRANSYT was first developed by Robertson but was substantially extended and enhanced later. It is the most known and most frequently applied signal control strategy, and it is often used as a reference method to test improvements enabled by real-time strategies. First field implementations of TRANSYT-produced signal plans indicated savings of some 16% of the average travel time through the network.

Figure 4.4 depicts the method's basic structure: TRANSYT is fed with the initial signal settings including the prespecified staging, the minimum green durations for each stage of each intersection, and the initial choice of splits, offsets, and cycle time. A unique cycle time is considered for all network intersections in order to enable offset coordination. The network and traffic flow data comprise the network's geometry, the saturation flows, the link travel times, the constant and known turning rates for each intersection, and the constant and known demands. The traffic model consists of nodes (intersections) and links (connecting streets). The concept of "platoon dispersion" (dynamic first-order time-delay system) is used to model flow progression along a link. Oversaturated conditions cannot be described, although some improvement has been achieved in this respect in a recent enhanced release of the program. The method proceeds in an iterative way:

For given values of the decision variables (control inputs), i.e., of splits, offsets, and cycle time, the dynamic network model calculates the corresponding performance index, e.g., the total number of vehicle stops. A heuristic "hill-climb" optimization algorithm introduces small changes to the decision variables and orders a new model run, and so forth, until a (local) minimum is found.

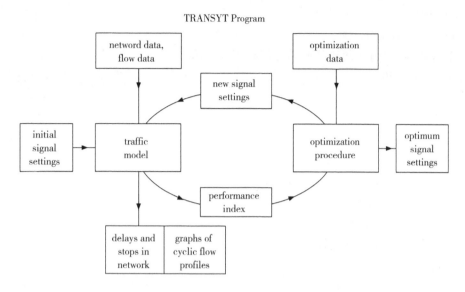

Figure 4.4 Structure of TRANSYT

Drawbacks of Fixed-Time Strategies: The main drawback of fixed-time strategies is that their settings are based on historical rather than real-time data. This may be a crude simplification for the following reasons.

- Demands are not constant, even within a time-of-day.
- Demands may vary at different days, e.g., due to special events.
- Demands change in the long term leading to "aging" of the optimized settings.
- Turning movements are also changing in the same ways as demands; in addition, turning movements may change due to the drivers' response to the new optimized signal settings, whereby they try to minimize their individual travel times.
- Incidents and farther disturbances may perturb traffic conditions in a nonpredictable way.

For all these reasons, traffic-responsive coordinated strategies, if suitably designed, are potentially more efficient, but also more costly, as they require the installation, operation, and maintenance of a real-time control system (sensors, communications, central control room, local controllers).

Vocabulary and Glossary

1. antagonistic *adj.* 敌对的;对抗性的
2. beacon *n.* 信标
3. branch-and-bound　[计]分支定界
4. compatible *adj.* 可以并存的,相容的,协调的
5. conflict *n.* 冲突
6. intersection *n.* 十字交叉口

7. MUTCD 美国标志标线标准
8. pedestrian *n.* 行人
9. phase-based 基于最小二阶差分的相展开方法
10. ramp *n.* 匝道
11. real-time 实时
12. right-of-way 路权
13. sigset 系统调用
14. traffic-responsive 交通感应
15. At-Grade intersection 平面交叉口
16. lost time 损失或延误的时间
17. signal phase 信号相位
18. traffic markings 交通标线
19. traffic signs 交通标志
20. traffic signals 交通信号

Exercises

I. True or false.

1. There are three broad categories for traffic control devices: traffic markings, traffic signs and traffic signals. ( )

2. Warning signs are used to inform drivers about upcoming hazards that they might not see or otherwise discern in time to safely react. ( )

3. At-Grade intersection is an intersection where two or more highways meet at the different levels. ( )

4. At an intersection level I control means basic rules of the road. ( )

5. Imposition of traffic signal control can remove all conflicts from the realm of driver judgment. ( )

II. Translate the following sentences into Chinese.

1. Traffic control devices are the media by which traffic engineers communicate with drivers.

2. Traffic markings serve a variety of purposes and functions and fall into three broad categories: longitudinal markings, transverse markings, object markers and delineators.

3. The critical task of traffic signal control of intersection is to manage the conflicts occurred at intersection in a manner that ensures safety and provides for efficient movement through the intersection for both motorists and pedestrians.

4. Even if sight distances are safe for operating under no control, there may be other reasons to implement a higher level of control as well.

5. Because it alternately assigns right-of-way to specific movements, it can substantially reduce the number and nature of intersection conflicts as no other form of control can.

6. Approaches vary with relative vehicular and pedestrian flow, but every signal timing must consider and provide for the requirements of both groups.

III. Discussions.

1. Talk about the categories of traffic markings.
2. How many categories traffic signs included.
3. Discuss the conflicts at a typical intersection of two two-way street.
4. Describing the key elements in signal design and timing

Reading Material: Traffic Signal Control Systems

Traffic-signal control systems coordinate individual traffic signals to achieve network-wide traffic operations objectives. These systems consist of intersection traffic signals, a communications network to tie them together, and a central computer or network of computers to manage the system. Coordination can be implemented through a number of techniques including time-base and hardwired interconnection methods. Coordination of traffic signals across agencies requires the development of data sharing and traffic signal control agreements. Therefore, a critical institutional component of Traffic Signal Control is the establishment of formal or informal arrangements to share traffic control information as well as actual control of traffic signal operation across jurisdictions.

Signal coordination systems are installed to provide access. A traffic-signal system has no other purpose than to deliver favorable signal timings to motorists. The system provides features that improve the traffic engineer's ability to achieve this goal. These are primarily access features. They provide access to the intersection signal controller for maintenance and operations. The more complete and convenient the access, the more efficient the operator will be and the more effective the system.

In addition to control traffic signals, modern systems also provide wide-ranging surveillance capabilities, including various kinds of traffic detection and video surveillance. They also provide more powerful traffic-control algorithms, including the potential for adaptive control and predictive surveillance.

Surface street control systems provide the majority of traffic-signal system applications. They are intended solely to provide control of networks of signal-controlled streets. When traffic-signal systems are integrated with freeway-management systems, their objectives take on a larger perspective.

Mainframe and UTCS Type Systems

In 1997, FHWA began development of the Urban Traffic Control Systems (UTCS) project.

The system was installed in Washington, DC, and was used to develop, test, and evaluate advanced traffic-control strategies. The system contained 512 vehicle detectors whose outputs were used to determine signal timings at 200 intersections. Extensive data processing, communications, and display capabilities were made available to support the traffic-control strategy research. Later research efforts produced Extended and Enhanced versions of the software package that implements these concepts.

Virtually all mainframe traffic-control systems in operation in the United States are based on one of two UTCS packages, originally supported and distributed by the FHWA. The Extended UTCS package, which uses a menu-type user interface, is considered by many to be the benchmark program against which features of competing programs are measured. The other package is the Enhanced package, originally developed by the FHWA to overcome shortcomings of the Extended package and to add additional features.

The enhanced UTCS package was completed and demonstrated in Birmingham, AL, in 1983. Versions of the Enhanced package have been installed in Los Angeles and San Diego, CA.

Closed-Loop Systems

The closed-loop system is a distributed processor traffic-control system with control logic distributed among three levels: the local controller, the on-street master, and the office computer. These systems provide two-way communication between the local controller(s) and the on-street master(s) and between the on-street master(s) and the central computer. Typically, the local controller receives information from field devices (e.g., system detectors). The master controller receives information (e.g., traffic and/or internal diagnostics) from the local controller. The central computer enables the system operator to monitor and control the system's operations.

One major disadvantage of the closed-loop system is unable to control intersections connected to different local area masters in a unified manner. This restriction precludes extensive reconfiguring of control area boundaries in response to differentiate traffic conditions.

Three control modes are typically found with most closed-loop systems: time of day, manual, and traffic responsive. With the time-of-day mode, the controller unit can automatically select and implement a prespecified traffic-signal timing plan and sequence (cycle/offset/split) based on the time of day, day of week, and/or time of year. With the manual mode, the operator specifies the pattern number of the desired traffic-signal timing plan and sequence via the computer console. With the traffic-responsive mode, the computer automatically selects the predefined traffic-signal timing plan best suited to accommodate the current traffic flow conditions in the signal network. The pattern selection and implementation is accomplished through a traffic flow data matching technique executed every five minutes on the five-minute mark.

Two other control modes have been used by some closed-loop systems: the controller unit parameter mode and the critical intersection control mode.

The closed-loop system consists of six components:

- System detectors;
- Local control equipment;
- Controller-master communications;
- On-street master;
- Master-central communications, and
- Central computer.

Traffic-Adaptive Signal Control

SCOOT

SCOOT (Split, Cycle, Offset Optimization Technique) is the premiere centralized adaptive control scheme available. The fundamental technology of SCOOT grew from the development of the Traffic Network Study Tool (TRANSYT) in the late 1970s and early 1980s, and was developed in the United Kingdom by the Transport and Road Research Laboratory (now the Transport Research Laboratory).

SCOOT performs optimization at three levels. SCOOT measures vehicles at a detector ideally placed at least eight seconds of travel time upstream from the stop line. Every second, the central program predicts the profile of arrivals to the signal based on the profile measured at the detector. This arrival profile is compared with a departure profile based on saturation occupancy from onset of green to clearance of the queue. The lapse between departure and arrival profiles represent those vehicles delayed in a queue. These profiles are measures of a combination of detector occupancy and gaps, called link profile units. Determination of these units is one of the secrets of SCOOT.

The split optimizer in SCOOT evaluates the projected arrival and departure profiles every second. Five seconds before each change of signals within the cycle, SCOOT adds the delay from all movements that will end or begin at that change of signals. This delay is compared against delay calculated with the change of signals occurring either four seconds earlier or four seconds later. Of the three, the scenario that provides the best balance of delay for the movements being optimized will be implemented. Evaluation of this balance is controlled by user-defined preferences. To track trends, SCOOT will carry over one second of the four-second adjustment to subsequent changes of the signals, although the offset optimizer may make further adjustments.

At the beginning of the interval serving a user-designated combination of traffic movements, the offset optimizer projects the delay for all the movements of that intersection, based on the profiles measured in the previous cycle. This interval is called the named, or nominated, interval. SCOOT may adjust all the signal change times for that cycle four seconds sooner, four seconds later, or not at all. After this offset adjustment, the split optimizer may further adjust these signal changes based on profiles actually approaching the stop line at that time.

The cycle optimizer looks at the saturation levels of all intersection movements once each cycle-control period (2.5 or 5 minutes). The intersection with the highest saturation is considered the critical intersection. If the saturation of the heaviest movements at the intersection exceeds 90 percent, the cycle optimizer will add 4, 8, or 16 seconds to the cycle depending on the length of the cycle (4 seconds for the shortest cycles, and 16 seconds for the longest cycles). If the saturation is much less than 90 percent, the cycle optimizer will subtract the increment from the cycle. Because cycle adjustments are kept very small, they can always be accommodated immediately within a few following signal intervals, and lengthy transition periods are therefore not needed. The cycle adjustment will be added to the named interval; therefore, the named interval should be the longest and most easily varied interval in the cycle (usually main-street through movements).

Setting up a SCOOT system first involves calibrating a range of parameters for each traffic movement in the network to ensure that the SCOOT model is working properly. These parameter adjustments require about the same level of effort during initial installation as conventional signal-timing calculations.

Once the movements are being properly modeled, the ranges within which the optimizers may work are defined, such as minimum and maximum cycle length, minimum movement timing, optimization preferences, etc.

SCOOT provides no optimization of phase sequence, although the systems that implement SCOOT allow complete flexibility in changing phase sequences by plan. SCOOT can then be used within these plans to provide adaptive control.

SCOOT detectors should be placed at least eight seconds of travel time upstream from the stop line, where possible to allow the link profile units to be measured before the split optimizer performs its duty. Typically, these detectors are placed on the outbound lanes of upstream intersections, and tied to the upstream intersection cabinet. The assignment of a SCOOT detector for the downstream intersection is made within SCOOT.

SCOOT is a centralized algorithm based on once-per-second mandatory communication with the local intersection controller. None of the optimization steps is performed in the local controller. Consequently, the SCOOT optimizer is wholly dependent on the communications network and central computer for operation.

SCATS

Sydney Coordinated Area Traffic System was developed by the Roads and Traffic Authority of New South Wales, Australia, and utilizes a distributed, three-level, hierarchical system using microprocessors and minicomputers. The system architecture consists of a central monitoring computer at the central control center, remote regional computers, and local traffic-signal controllers.

For large systems with more than 400 signals, a VAX computer is recommended to provide system management support, data collection and analysis, data backup, fault analysis, and system inventory facilities. The central monitoring computer allows access to the regional computers for traffic data collection, data input, and monitoring. It performs the following functions without influencing traffic operation:

- Outputs traffic and equipment status for fault rectification.

- Stores specific traffic data for short-term or permanent record.
- Maintains the core image for each regional computer, and reloads the regional computer if required.
- Allows central control to monitor system, subsystem, or intersection, alter control parameters, manually override dynamic functions, or plot time-distance diagrams.

Each regional computer autonomously controls the intersections in its area. These computers are the heart of the SCATS system. They are usually installed at the center of the groups of traffic signals to be controlled in order to reduce the cost of the communications. They implement the signals by analysis of the detector information preprocessed by the local microprocessors.

The local controller, at the traffic-signal site, processes data collected from traffic detectors, makes tactical decisions on signal operation, and assesses detector performance. It also incorporates a software method of cableless link coordination (with 11 plans) through synchronous clocks. This provides a fall-back mode of operation that enhances total system security without the need for dual computer systems.

Chapter 5   Traffic Planning

➔ Text A   What Will Our Community Look Like in the Future?

Transportation has significant effects on land use, mobility, economic development, environmental quality, government finance and the quality of life. Wise planning is needed to help create high quality transportation services at a reasonable cost with minimal environmental impact. Failure to plan can lead to severe traffic congestion, dangerous travel patterns, undesirable land use patterns, adverse environmental impact and wasteful use of money and resources.

Before forecasts are made of travel, it is necessary to develop forecast of future population, economic activity and land use. Transportation planning is directly linked to land use planning. Trips are assumed to follow future land use patterns. If land use is changed, there will be a change in travel patterns.

How many people will there be? (population forecasts)

Future population forecasts are based on assumptions about birth rates, death rates and the rate of migration into and out of the study area. Current information about the ages of the population is used to forecast ahead by the calculation of the number of births, deaths and migrants added and leaving the region in each year of the future. These rates are assumed to remain constant or to change in a specified way. These rates have changed substantially over the past 30 years so often several forecasts are made under different growth rate assumptions.

What activities will people engage in? (economic forecasts)

Forecasts need to be made of future employment levels as these are the basis for forecasts of travel to work, school, shopping, etc. Economic forecasts are done in conjunction with the population forecasts since the two are highly interrelated. Employment grows because the population is growing, but migration rates into and out of the community depend upon the growth of the economy. Assumptions have to be made of the ability of a region to generate new basic employment and to hold onto its existing basic employment. Basic employment is that which exports good and service outside of the region. It is different from the non-basic or local sector of the economy which circulates the money brought into a region by the basic sector. Total employment is found by applying an economic multiplier to basic employment.

Where will activities occur? (land use)

Population and economic growth has to be distributed to different locations in order to do travel forecasts. It is necessary to know where people will live, work, shop and go to school in the future to estimate of future trip making. Future allocation of land use may be based on past trends, assumptions about changes in trends or through a negotiation process among local officials. Land use plans are developed to change existing trends if is felt that current trends will not continue or are undesirable.

The first step in a land use planning process is to establish specific land use goals and associated land use rates. Goals need to be set concerning preservation of open space, wetlands and environmental corridors as well as land use mixes and densities. Quantities of land required for various uses are established to meet projections of population and employment. Alternative plans can be developed to reflect different goals, land use policies and assumptions. For example, land use plans could be developed to continue current trends, to reduce low density urban development, or to concentrate development along major corridors or in satellite communities. Different assumptions could be made regarding the extent to which environmentally sensitive areas and prime agricultural land will be protected. It is important to understand that land use and transportation are highly interrelated. The typical process uses the land use plan to determine the transportation plan. However, transportation has a major effect on land use and should be considered when a land use plan is developed.

Once the quantities of land needed are known for the future, it must be allocated to specific locations. A regional allocation is important since local communities often overestimate their growth. Individual community zoning often allocates far more commercial and industrial land use than may be necessary when looked at from a regional perspective. Land use allocation can be done either through a judgement technique or through a modeling process. The judgement technique involves the allocation of growth in steps to smaller and smaller geographic areas considering past trends, availability of open land for future potential development and local plans and zoning ordinances. It is sometimes done with the use of an expert panel that includes local planners, developers, financiers and real estate brokers. An allocation is made by following rules and guidelines as established from the land use goals.

A modeling approach to land use allocation can be used to determine the impact of transportation facilities on growth patterns. The locations of basic employment are set by hand and the model locates other employment and residential land use in relationship to the basic employment. Allocations are determined based on the availability of open land and upon the accessibility that is provided from a proposed transportation plan. The modeling process finds a balance between supply and demand for both land use and transportation. As such it indicates how land use change is driven by changes in the transportation system. This can be helpful in that it could indicate undesirable trends and/or suggest policies to avoid them. This approach is relatively new and has only been used in limited locations.

Common limitations and issues: some of the common limitations which could be of concern in the land use planning process are the following.

(1) No feedback with transportation plans. Common practice is that land use plans are developed before transportation plans and assumed not to change as a result of the transportation improvements. This is especially common in the preparation of environmental impact statements and highway location studies.

(2) Current development is fixed. Land use plans generally only deal with new growth on vacant land and assume that current development will be unchanged. Effects of redevelopment programs, changing use of neighborhoods and so forth are normally not considered.

(3) Mixed use benefits are not considered. Land use patterns that facilitate walking and non automobile travel are not easily dealt with in the modelling process and generally not considered.

➡ Text B What Are the Travel Patterns in the Future?

The travel forecasting process is at the heart of urban transportation planning. Travel forecasting models are used to project future traffic and are the basis for the determination of the need for new road capacity, transit service changes and changes in land use policies and patterns. Travel demand modeling involves a series of mathematical models that attempt to simulate human behavior while traveling. The models are done in a sequence of steps that answer a series of questions about traveler decisions. Attempts are made to simulate all choices that travelers make in response to a given system of highways, transit and policies. Many assumptions need to be made about how people make decisions, the factors they consider and how they react to a particular transportation alternative.

The travel simulation process follows trips as they begin at a trip generation zone, move through a network of links and nodes and end at a trip attracting zone. The simulation process is known as the four step process for the four basic models used. These are: trip generation, trip distribution, mode split and traffic assignments. These models are used to answer a series of questions as explained in the remainder of the primer. In addition the process used to represent urban areas and the use of model results will also be described.

How is the city represented for computer analysis? (zone/network system)

Travel simulations require that an urban area be represented as a series of small geographic areas called travel analysis zones (TAZs). Zones are characterized by their population, employment and other factors and are the places where trips begin (trip producers) or end (trip attractors). Trip making is first estimated at the household level and then aggregated to the zone level. Trip making is assumed to begin at the center of activity in a zone (zone centroid). Trips that are very short, that begin and end in a single zone (intrazonal trips) are usually not directly included in the forecasts. This limits the analysis of pedestrian and bicycle trips in the typical travel demand modeling process since they tend to be short trips.

Zones can be as small as a single block but typically are 1/4 to one mile square in area. A planning study can easily use 500-2000 zones. A large number of zones will increase forecast accuracy but will require more data and computer processing time. Zones tend to be small in areas of high population and larger in more rural areas. Internal zones are those within the study area while external zones are those outside of the study area. The study area should be large enough so that nearly all (over 90%) of the trips begin and end within the study area.

The highway system and transit systems are represented as networks for computer analysis. Networks consist of links to represent highways' segments or transit lines and nodes to represent intersections and other points on the network. Data for links includes travel times on the link, average speeds, capacity, and direction. Node data includes information about intersections and the location of the node (coordinates).

How many trips will there be? (trip generation)

The first step in travel forecasting is trip generation. In this step information from land use, population and economic forecasts are used to estimate how many person trips will be made to and from each zone. This is done separately by trip purpose. Trip purposes that can be used include: home based work trips (work trips that begin or end at home), home based shopping trips, home based other trips, school trips, non-home based trips (trips that neither begin nor end at home), truck trips and taxi trips. Trip generation uses trip rates that are averages for large segment of the study area. Trip productions are based on household characteristics such as the number of people in the household and the number of vehicles available. For example, a household with four people and two vehicles may be assumed to produce 3.00 work trips per day. Trips per household are then expanded to trips per zone. Trip attractions are typically based on the level of employment in a zone. For example a zone could be assumed to attract 1.32 home based work trips for every person employed in that zone. Trip generation is used to calculate person trips. These are later adjusted in the mode split/auto occupancy step to determine vehicle trips.

How do the trip ends connect together? (trip distribution)

Trip generation only finds the number of trips that begin or end at a particular zone. These trip ends are linked together to form an origin-destination pattern of trips through the process of trip distribution. Trip distribution is used to represent the process of destination choice, i.e. "I need to go shopping but where should I go to meet my shopping needs?". Trip distribution leads to a large increase in the amount of data which needs to be dealt with. Origin-destination tables are very large. For example a 1200 zone study area would have a 1,440,000 possible trip combinations in its O-D table. Separate tables are also done for each trip purpose.

The most commonly used procedure for trip distribution is the "gravity model". The gravity model takes the trips produced at one zone and distributes to other zones based on the size of the other zones (as measured by their trip attractions) and on the basis of the distance to other zones. A zone with a large number of trip attractions will receive a greater number of distributed trips than one with a small number of trip attractions. Distance to possible destinations is the other factor used in the gravity model. The number of trips to a given destination decreases with the distance to the destination (it is inversely proportional). The distance effect is found through a calibration process which tries to lead to a distribution of trips from the model similar to that found from field data.

"Distance" can be measured several ways. The simplest way that is done is to use auto travel times between zones as the measurement of distance. Other ways might be to use a combination of auto travel time and cost as the measurement of distance. Still another way is to use a combination of transit and auto times and costs (composite cost). This method involves using multiplying auto travel times and costs by a percentage and transit time/cost another percentage to get a composite time and cost of both modes. Because of calculation procedures, the model must be iterated a number of times in order to balance the trip numbers to match the trip productions and attractions found in trip generation.

How will people travel? (mode choice/auto occupancy analysis)

Mode choice is one of the most critical parts of the travel demand modeling process. It is the step where trips between a given origin and destination are split into trips using transit, trips by car pool or as automobile passengers and trips by automobile drivers. Calculations are conducted that compare the attractiveness of travel by different modes to determine their relative usage. All proposals to improve public transit or to change the ease of using the automobile are passed through the mode split/auto occupancy process as part of their assessment and evaluation. It is important to understand what factors are used and how the process is conducted in order to plan, design and implement new systems of transportation.

The most commonly used process for mode split is to use the "Logit" model. This involves a comparison of the "disutility" of travel between two points for the different modes that are available. Disutility is a term used to represent a combination of the travel time, cost and convenience of a mode between an origin and a destination. It is found by placing multipliers (weights) on these factors and adding them together. Travel time is divided into two components: in-vehicle time to represent the time when a traveler is actually in a vehicle and out-of-vehicle time which includes time spent traveling which occurs outside of the vehicle (time to walk to and from transit stops or parking places, waiting time, transfer time). Out-of-vehicle time is used to represent "convenience" and is typically multiplied by a factor of 2.0 to 7.0 to give it a greater importance in the calculations. This is because travelers do not like to wait or walk long distances to their destinations. The size of the multiplier will be different depending upon the purpose of the trip. This is because it has been found that people tend to be more willing to wait or walk longer distances for work trips than for shopping trips.

Travel cost is multiplied by a factor to represent the value that travelers place on time savings for a particular trip purpose. For transit trips, the cost of the trip is given as the average transit fare for that trip while for auto trips cost is found by adding the parking cost to the length of the trip as multiplied by a cost per mile. Auto cost is based on a "perceived" cost per mile (on the order of 5-7 cents/mile) which only includes fuel and oil costs and does not include ownership, insurance, maintenance and other fixed costs (total costs of automobile travel are 25-40 cents per mile). Travelers have been found to only consider the costs that vary with an individual trip rather than all costs when making mode choice decisions.

Disutility calculations may also contain a "mode bias factor" which is used to represent other characteristics or travel modes which may influence the choice of mode (such as a difference in privacy and comfort between transit and automobiles). The mode bias factor is used as a constant in the analysis and is found by attempt to fit the model to actual travel behavior data. Generally, the disutility equations do not recognize differences within travel modes. For example, a bus system and a rail system with the same time and cost characteristics will have the same disutility values. There are no special factors that allow for the difference in attractiveness of alternative technologies.

Once disutilities are known for the various mode choices between an origin and a destination, the trips are split among various modes based on the relative differences between disutilities. The logit equation is used in this step. A large advantage in disutility will mean a high percentage for that mode. Mode splits are calculated to match splits found from actual traveler data. Sometimes a fixed percentage is used for the minimum transit use (percent captive users) to represent travelers who have no automobile available or are unable to use an automobile for their trip.

Automobile trips must be converted from person trips to vehicle trips with an auto occupancy model. Mode split and auto occupancy analysis can be two separate steps or can be combined into a single step, depending on how a forecasting process is set up. In the simplest application a highway/transit split is made first which is followed by a split of automobile trips into auto driver and auto passenger trips. More complex analysis splits trips into multiple categories (single occupant auto, two person car pool, 3-5 person car pool, van pool, local bus, express bus, etc.). Auto occupancy analysis is often a highly simplified process which uses fixed auto occupancy rates for a given trip purpose or for given household size and auto ownership categories. This means that the forecasts of car pooling are insensitive to changes in the cost of travel, the cost of parking, the presence of special programs to promote car pooling.

What routes will be used? (traffic assignment)

Once trips have been split into highway and transit trips, the specific path that they use to travel from their origin to their destination must be found. These trips are then assigned to that path in the step called traffic assignment. Traffic assignment is the most time consuming and data intensive step in the process and is done differently for highway trips and transit trips. The process first involves the calculation of the shortest path from each origin to all destinations (usually the minimum time path is used). Trips for each O-D pair are then assigned to the links in the minimum path and the trips are added up for each link. The assigned trip volume is then compared to the capacity of the link to see if it is congested. If a link is congested the speed on the link needs to be reduced to result in a longer travel time on that link. Changes in travel times means that the shortest path may change. Hence the whole process is repeated several times (iterated) until there is an equilibrium between travel demand and travel supply. Trips on congested links will be shifted to uncongested links until this equilibrium, condition occurs. Traffic assignment is the most complex calculation in the travel modeling sequence and there are a variety of ways in which it is done to keep computer time to a minimum.

Transit trip assignment is done in a similar way to auto trip assignment except that transit headways are adjusted rather than travel times. Transit headways (minutes between vehicles) affect the capacity of a transit route. Short headways mean more frequent service and a greater number of vehicles. Normally short headways are assumed initially. Trips are assigned to vehicles and if the vehicles have low ridership, headways are increased to provide fewer vehicles and higher ridership per trip. This process is repeated until transit supply and demand are in balance.

It is important to understand the concept of equilibrium. If a highway or transit route is congested during the peak hour, its excess trips will shift to other routes, to other destinations to other modes or to other times of day. Increases in capacity will cause shifts back to the facility to reach a new equilibrium point. Furthermore it may also lead to additional trip making in the form of "induced" trips. These would be trips that did not take place before the facility was expanded. The new equilibrium may mean that the congestion is reestablished on the facility.

Considerations of time of day are also important. Traffic assignment is typically done for peak hour travel while forecasts of trips are done on a daily basis. A ratio of peak hour travel to daily travel is needed to convert daily trips to peak hour travel (for example it may be assumed that ten percent of travel occurs in the peak hour). Numbers used for this step are very important in that a small change in the values assumed will make a considerable difference in the level of congestion forecasted on a network. Normally the modeling process does not deal with how traffic congestion dissipates over time.

What are the effects of the travel?

Equilibrium traffic assignment results indicate the amount of travel to be expected on each link in the network at some future date with a given transportation system. Levels of congestion, travel times, speed of travel and vehicle miles of travel i. e. VMT are direct outputs from the modeling process. Link traffic volumes are also used to determine other effects of travel for plan evaluation. Some of the key effects are accidents, and estimates of air pollution emissions. Each of these effects needs to be estimated through further calculations. Typically these are done by applying accident or emission rates by highway type and by speed. Assumptions need to be made of the speed characteristics of travel for non-peak hours of the day and for variation in travel by time of the year.

Vocabulary and Glossary

1. community *n.* 社区,社会,群落
2. equilibrium *n.* 平衡,均势
3. ridership *n.* 公共交通的客流量
4. transit *n.* 公共交通
5. VMT vehicle miles traveled 车辆的行程里数
6. car pool 合乘
7. data collection 数据采集
8. expert panel 专家组
9. four step process 四阶段法
10. gravity model 重力模型
11. highway planning 道路规划
12. home based trips and non-home based trips 基于家出行与非基于家出行
13. households interview 家访调查
14. land use planning 土地利用规划
15. link and routes 路段与路径
16. mode choice 方式选择
17. mode split 方式划分
18. multimodal planning 多运输方式交通规划
19. out-of-vehicle time and in-vehicle time 车外时间与车内时间
20. rate of migration 迁移率,分为迁出率和迁入率
21. satellite communities 卫星城(区)
22. supply and demand 供给与需求
23. traffic analysis zones 交通分析小区
24. traffic assignments 交通分配
25. traffic congestion 交通拥堵
26. traffic consensus 交通调查
27. traffic corridors 交通走廊
28. traffic mode 交通方式
29. traffic planning 交通规划
30. transit headways 公交车头距离

31. travel demand   交通需求
32. travel forecast   交通出行预测
33. trip distribution   出行分布
34. trip generation   出行生成
35. trip production and trip attraction   出行发生与吸引
36. urban transportation planning   城市交通规划
37. waiting time and transfer time   等待时间与换乘时间

Exercises

I. True or false.

1. Future population forecasts are based on birth rates, death rates and the rate of migration into the study area.　　　　　　　　　　　　　　　　　　　　　　　　　　　　(　)

2. The purpose of the economic forecasts is to find future employment levels as these are the basis for forecasts of travel to work, school, shopping, etc.　　　　　　　　(　)

3. Future allocation of land use is to know where people will live, work, shop and go to school in the future.　　　　　　　　　　　　　　　　　　　　　　　　　　　　(　)

4. The travel forecasting is the four-step process of urban transportation planning.　(　)

5. For travel analysis, zones should be the smaller, the better.　　　　　　　　　(　)

6. Trip generation is to estimate how many person trips will be produced from and attracted to each zone.　　　　　　　　　　　　　　　　　　　　　　　　　　　　　(　)

II. Translate the following sentences into Chinese.

1. Wise planning is needed to help create high quality transportation services at a reasonable cost with minimal environmental impact. Failure to plan can lead to severe traffic congestion, dangerous travel patterns, undesirable land use patterns, adverse environmental impact and wasteful use of money and resources.

2. Future population forecasts are based on assumptions about birth rates, death rates and the rate of migration into or out of the study area.

3. Allocations are determined based on the availability of open land and upon the accessibility that is provided from a proposed transportation plan.

4. Common practice is that land use plans are developed before transportation plans and assumed to not change as a result of the transportation improvements.

5. Travel forecasting models are used to project future traffic and are the basis for the determination of the need for new road capacity, transit service changes and changes in land use policies and patterns.

6. The gravity model takes the trips produced at one zone and distributes to other zones based

on the size of the other zones (as measured by their trip attractions) and on the basis of the distance to other zones.

7. For transit trips, the cost of the trip is given as the average transit fare for that trip while for auto trips cost is found by adding the parking cost to the length of the trip as multiplied by a cost per mile.

8. Trips for each O-D pair are assigned to the links in the minimum time path and the trips are added up for each link. The assigned trip volume is then compared to the capacity of the link to see if it is congested. If a link is congested the speed on the link needs to be reduced to result in a longer travel time on that link. Changes in travel times means that the shortest path may change. Trips on congested links will be shifted to uncongested links until this equilibrium, condition occurs.

III. Discussions.

1. What is the use of land use forecasting?
2. What does a traffic network include?
3. What is the demonstration for trip distribution?
4. In the traffic demand forecasting, are there only one O-D table we need to use?
5. What's the result of the mode choice process?
6. Can you express the "disutility" function?
7. What is the direct output of traffic assignment process?
8. What is the direct outputs of the four steps?

Reading Material: Why are Planning Models Important?

Transportation planning uses the term "models" extensively. This term is used to refer to a series of mathematical equations that are used to represent how choices are made when people travel. Travel demand occurs as a result of thousands of individual travelers making individual decisions on how, where and when to travel. These decisions are affected by many factors such as family situations, characteristics of the person making the trip, and the choices (destination, route and mode) available for the trip. Mathematical relationships are used to represent (model) human behavior in making these choices. Models require a series of assumptions in order to work and are limited by the data available to make forecasts. The coefficients and parameters in the model are set (calibrated) to match existing data. Normally, these relationships are assumed to be valid and to remain constant in the future.

Travel demand modeling was first developed in the late 1950's as a means to do highway planning. As the need to look at other problems such as transit, land use issues and air quality analysis arose, the modeling process has been modified to add additional techniques to deal with these problems.

Models are important because transportation plans and investments are based on what the models say about future travel. Models are used to estimate the number of trips that will be made on a transportation systems alternative at some future date. These estimates are the basis for transportation plans and are used in major investment analysis, environmental impact statements and in setting priorities for investments. Models are based upon assumptions of the way in which travel occurs. A clear understanding of the modeling process is important to help to understand transportation plans and their recommendations.

Transportation modeling is used to develop information to help make decisions on the future development and management of transportation systems, especially in urban areas. It is used as part of an overall transportation planning process which involves a forecast of travel patterns 15 to 25 years into the future and an attempt to develop a future transportation system that will work effectively in the future. Transportation has significant effects on land use, mobility, economic development, environmental quality, government finance and the quality of life. Wise planning is needed to help create high quality transportation services at a reasonable cost with minimal environmental impact. Failure to plan can lead to severe traffic congestion, dangerous travel patterns, undesirable land use patterns, adverse environmental impact and wasteful use of money and resources. Significant transportation projects require a long lead time for their design and construction.

What is the legal basis for transportation planning?

Transportation planning is required in the United States as a condition to receive federal transportation funds for larger urban areas. Requirements for urban transportation planning were first enacted in legislation passed on 1962. These have been expanded and modified in subsequent legislation, most recently through the Intermodal Surface Transportation Efficiency Act of 1991 (ISTEA) and the Transportation Efficiency Act (TEA-21). ISTEA specifically listed 15 factors that must be considered in urban transportation planning. These factors have led to planning regulations that require planning agencies to deal with air quality issues, multimodal planning, better management of existing systems, expanded public input and financial analysis requirements. Generally they have led to a greater role for transportation planning in urban areas, especially with a need to consider a wider range of alternatives and consequences of transportation investment choices.

How do models fit into the overall transportation planning process?

Transportation planning is a complex process that involves a basic sequence of steps. Several can take place at once and it is not unusual to repeat some of the steps several times. Travel demand models are used in the forecasting step of the process as the means to predict how well alternative plans perform in meeting goals. The basic steps in the transportation planning process are the following:

Problem definition: This step identifies the key transportation, socio-economic and land use issues and problems facing the community. This step may also involve definition of the size of an area to be studied, determination of the scope of the study and the establishment of a committee structure to oversee the planning process.

Define goals, objectives and criteria: A consensus should be developed by elected officials and citizens about the future of the community and its transportation system. Goals are developed for the quality of transportation service, environmental impacts and costs. Some of these will likely be in conflict. A good planning effort will identify the trade-offs between these factors among alternatives in a clear, concise way to help make decisions. Along with goals it is important to identify more specific objectives and criteria which can be used to specifically measure how well alternative plans perform in meeting the more general goals.

Data collection: Data must be compiled about the present status of the transportation system and its use. This could include traffic data, transit ridership statistics, census information and interviews of households about their travel patterns. Data are also gathered on land use, development trends, environmental factors, and financial resources. This will assist in problem definition and in developing methods to forecast future travel patterns. Good data are essential to the planning process. The statement "garbage in/garbage out" applies in transportation planning. Without good data, the results of the planning process have little real meaning and can lead to the wrong projects selected and a wrong direction for the region.

Forecasts (modeling): Data from existing travel is used to make forecasts of future travel using travel demand models. This requires forecasts of future land use and economic conditions as well as understanding of how people make travel choices. Forecasting requires large amounts of data and is done under many assumptions.

Develop alternatives: Forecasts are used to determine the performance of alternative future land use and transportation systems. Alternatives normally include different land use and transportation systems and mixtures of highway and transit services and facilities. Since land use affects travel and travel affects land use, both must be considered.

Evaluation: Results of forecasts are used to compare the performance of alternatives in meeting goals, objectives and criteria. This information may be extensively discussed by interested citizens, elected officials, different government agencies and the private sector. Ultimately decisions are made by appropriate elected or appointed groups for future transportation projects.

Implementation plan: Once decisions are made, plans should be further developed and refined for implementation. This may include more detailed analysis for design and evaluation following the same as process as above.

Chapter 6　Traffic Safety

➡ Text A　Introduction to Traffic Safety

More than a million people are killed on the world's roads each year. With the number of motor vehicles increases rapidly in many formerly less-motorized countries, the total fatalities are expected to increase steeply and and will likely exceed 2 million by the year 2020. Traffic crashes are one of the world's largest public health problems. The problem is all the more acute because the victims are overwhelmingly young and healthy prior to their crashes.

Fatalities on U.S. highways have reached more than 30,000 per year. In a typical month, more Americans die in traffic than were killed by the 11 September 2001 terrorist attacks on New York and Washington. The families of the traffic-crash victims receive no particular consideration or compensation from the nation or its major charitable organizations. Since the coming of the automobile in the early days of the twentieth century, more than three million Americans have been killed in traffic crashes, vastly more than the 650,000 American battle deaths in all wars, from the start of the revolutionary war in 1775 through the 2003 war in Iraq.

When 14 teenagers died in the 1999 Columbine High School shootings, much of the population of the US, led by President Clinton, grieved along with the bereaved families. Yet more teenagers are killed on a typical day in US traffic. In 2002, 5,933 people aged 13-19 were killed, which is an average of 16.3 teenagers killed per day. These deaths barely touch the nation's consciousness. Families bereaved by a traffic death are no less devastated than the Columbine families. Indeed, their burden may be even more unbearable as they do not receive the support provided to the Columbine families.

Injuries due to traffic crashes vastly outnumber fatalities, with over 5 million occurring per year in the US, most of them are minors. The number of injuries reported depends strongly on the level of injury included. Applying the US ratio of 120 injuries for each fatality implies about 120 million annual traffic injuries worldwide. Dividing this by the world population of 6 billion, implies that the average human being has a near two percent chance of being injured in traffic each year—more than a fifty percent chance in a lifetime.

Traffic crashes also damage property, especially vehicles. By converting all losses to monetary values, it is estimated that US traffic crashes in 2000 cost $231 billion, an amount greater than the Gross Domestic Product of all but a few countries.

Specialists and the public use the term safety widely. Such use rarely generates serious misunderstanding even though there is no precise, let alone quantitative, definition of safety. The general concept is the absence of unintended harm to living creatures or inanimate objects. Quantitative safety measures nearly always focus on the magnitudes of departures from perfect safety, rather than directly on safety as such. Depending on the specific subject and on available data, many measures have been used.

A feature that measures of safety have in common is that they are, in essentially all cases, rates. That is, some measure of harm (deaths, injuries, or property damage) divided by some indicator of exposure to the risk of this harm. For example, rates related to driver deaths include the number of driver deaths per kilometer of travel, per vehicle, per licensed driver, and per year. Note that the number of driver deaths per year is just as much a rate as any of the other examples.

Even within a narrow portion of transportation (say, scheduled airlines or motorcycles), there is no one rate that is superior to others in any general sense. Which rate is appropriate depends on what question is asked (and also on what data are available).

While safety is an important consideration in many human activities, it has a particularly prominent role in transportation. Every type of transportation system involves some risk of harm, as has been the case since antiquity, and seems likely to remain the case in the future. The primary goal of transportation, the effective movement of people and goods, is better served by ever increasing speeds. A substantial proportion of technological innovation for the last few thousand years has focused on increasing transportation speeds, from animal-powered to supersonic flight. In general, as speed increases so does risk.

➡ Text B Human Factors and Traffic Safety

Discussion of the influence of human factors of drivers (and of road users in general) on road safety must make the clearest distinction between two deceptively similar but fundamentally different concepts:
- Driver performance——what the driver can do, or is capable of doing?
- Driver behavior——what the driver in fact does?

Driver Performance

Studies have concluded that driving error is a contributory factor in over 95% of traffic crashes. Such findings have generated suggestions that the first priority for better safety is to teach higher levels of skill and knowledge about driving. That is, to improve levels of driver performance. While driver training, especially of motorcycle riders, has reduced crash rates in some cases, it has not generally been found to do so. A number of considerations show why crash risk is not determined mainly by driver performance.

Everywhere young male drivers have the highest crash rates. However this is the very age group with the best visual acuity, swiftest reaction times, and fastest cognitive processing skills. Males tend to be more knowledgeable about and interested in driving and automobiles. Racing-car drivers have higher on-the-road crash rates than average drivers. Much more important than what the driver can do is what the driver chooses to do.

Driver Behavior

The average driver has a crash about once per decade (usually a minor property damage crash—for fatal crashes it is about one per 4,000 years). Drivers tend to dismiss their crashes as unpredictable and unpreventable bad luck, or the other involved driver's fault. A more appropriate interpretation is that average driving produces one crash per ten years. Feedback once per decade is unlikely to affect behavior. Every crash-free trip reinforces the driver's incorrect conclusion that average driving is safe driving. Individual experience is a false teacher.

A crucial factor that contributes to the high level of commercial airline safety is that pilots follow procedures based on expert analyses of the experience of many. For road vehicles, traffic laws attempt to fulfill a parallel role. However, ground vehicle drivers routinely violate such laws.

Two of the factors, most affecting road-traffic fatality risk, are travel speed and alcohol consumption. Research indicates that the risk of crashing increases approximately in proportion to travel speed, injury risk in proportion to travel speed squared, and fatality risk in proportion to travel speed to the fourth power. When speed limits on the US rural intrastate system were reduced in 1974 from 70 mph to 55 mph following the October 1973 Arab oil embargo, average travel speed dropped from 63.4 mph to 57.6 mph. This change leads to a predicted fatality risk decrease of 32%, remarkably close to the 34% decline observed. Case-control studies found casualty crash to double with each 5 km/h increase in speed.

Drunk driving is a major traffic safety problem in all countries in which alcohol is used widely, often accounting for about half of all fatalities. Reducing the availability of alcohol has in many cases led to reduced traffic deaths. When all US states increased the minimum age to purchase or consume alcohol to 21 years, from earlier ages of 18 to 20 years in various states, a 13% reduction in fatal-crash involvements of affected drivers followed. Police use of random breath testing to enforce drunk driving laws more effectively has reduced casualties. The New South Wales state of Australian tests about a third of all drivers each year, many of them more than once. This intervention decreased overall fatalities by about 19%.

Driver behavior is a crucial factor in occupant protection because the most effective occupant protection device, the safety belt, works only when fastened. Mandatory wearing laws have been introduced in most countries, though wearing rates and level and type of enforcement vary greatly. The best evaluated wearing law was that for the United Kingdom, where fatality rates for drivers and left front passengers declined by about 20%.

Vehicles are used for purposes that go beyond transportation, including competitiveness, sense of power and control, or more generally, hedonistic objectives——the pursuit of sensual pleasure for its own sake. Speed and acceleration appear to produce pleasurable excitement even when no specific destination lies ahead and there is no point in haste. While most drivers are motivated by nontransportation motives at some times, as they mature the mix of motives evolves in a more utilitarian direction. This is likely one reason why crash risk is so much lower for 40-year-olds than for 20-year-olds. It seems plausible that as a nation's motorization matures, a similar evolution occurs and contributes to a lowering of crash rates. Drivers in newly motorized countries are likely to be the first generation to drive, and to approach the activity with a sense of novelty, excitement and adventure. In motorized countries, children grow up with the motor vehicle playing an essential role in even the most routine and mundane aspects of daily life.

Crash risk relates to the deepest human characteristics. Factors at the very core of human personality influence behavior in traffic. A comparison of the gender and age dependence of involvement rates in severe single-vehicle crashes and in crimes unrelated to traffic offenses (say, burglary, as a typical example) show remarkable similarities. No one would suggest seriously that 40-year-olds commit fewer burglaries than 20-year-olds solely because the 40-year-olds have learned how not to commit burglaries! This should invite a parallel caution against interpreting lower crash rates for 40-year-old drivers compared to those for 20-year-old drivers to mean that the 40-year-olds have simply learned how to not crash.

The dominant role of driver behavior. As discussed above, reducing the speed limit from 70 to 55 miles per hour reduced fatality rates on US rural interstate roads by 34%, mandatory safety-belt wearing in the United Kingdom reduced front-seat occupant fatalities by 20%, and random breath testing for alcohol in the Australian state of New South Wales reduced driver fatalities by 19%.

In the 1970s, major independent studies in the US and in Britain identified factors associated with large samples of crashes. The US study found the road user to be the sole factor in 57% of crashes, the roadway in 3%, and the vehicle in 2%; the corresponding values from the British study were 65%, 2% and 2% respectively. In nearly all cases the vehicular factor was in fact a vehicle maintenance problem, such as bald tires or worn brake linings. The road user was identified as a sole or contributing factor in 94% of crashes in the US study and in 95% of crashes in the British study.

Vocabulary and Glossary

1. acute *adj.* 尖的,锐的; 敏锐的,敏感的;严重的,剧烈的
2. antiquity *n.* 古老,古代;古迹,古物;古人;古代的风俗习惯
3. behavior *n.* 行为,举止;态度;反应

4. compensation *n.* 补偿;报酬;赔偿金

5. consciousness *n.* 意识;知觉;觉悟;感觉

6. contributory *adj.* 促成的;促进的;起作用的

7. crash *n.* 撞碎;坠毁

8. charitable *adj.* 仁慈的,慈善的;宽恕的,宽厚的;慷慨的

9. damage *v.* 损害,毁坏

10. devastate *v.* 破坏;毁灭;蹂躏;使荒废

11. fatality *n.* 灾祸;死亡(事故)

12. grieve *v.* 使伤心;使悲伤

13. hedonistic *adj.* 快乐主义者的

14. indicator *n.* 指示器;指示剂;指示符

15. mandatory *adj.* 强制的;命令的;受委托的

16. motorized *adj.* 摩托化的;机动化的

17. unbearable *adj.* 难以忍受的;承受不住的

18. outnumber *v.* 数目超过;比…多

19. overwhelmingly *adv.* 压倒性地;不可抵抗地

20. parallel *adj.* 相同的,类似的

21. performance *n.* 性能;表演;执行

22. prominent *adj.* 突出的,杰出的;突起的

23. quantitative *adj.* 定量的;数量(上)的

24. steeply *adv.* 大坡度地

25. supersonic *adj.* [物]超声的,超音速的

26. victim *n.* 受害人;牺牲品;牺牲者

27. visual *adj.* 视觉的,看得见的;光学的,视力的;形象化的;光学的

28. drunk driving 酒后驾驶

Exercises

I. True or false.

1. The families of the traffic-crash victims receive particular consideration or compensation from the nation or its major charitable organizations. ( )

2. Quantitative safety measures nearly always focus on the magnitudes of departures from perfect safety, rather than directly on safety as such. ( )

3. Every type of transportation system involves some risk of harm, as has been the case since antiquity, and seems likely to remain the case in the future. ( )

4. Such findings have generated suggestions that the first priority for better safety is to teach higher levels of skill and knowledge about driving. That is, to improve levels of driver behavior. ( )

5. A crucial factor that contributes to the high level of commercial airline safety is that pilots follow procedures based on expert analyses of the experience of many.　　　　(　　)

II. Choose the best word or phrase to complete each statement.

1. Dividing this by the world population of 6 billion, implies that the average human being has a near _____ percent chance of being injured in traffic each year—more than a fifty percent chance in a lifetime.

　　A. one　　　　　　B. two　　　　　　C. three　　　　　　D. four

2. A feature that measures of safety have in common is that they are, in essentially all cases, _____. That is, some measure of harm (deaths, injuries, or property damage) divided by some indicator of exposure to the risk of this harm.

　　A. speeds　　　　B. distances　　　　C. rates　　　　　D. times

3. Every crash-free trip reinforces the driver's incorrect conclusion that _____ driving is safe driving.

　　A. slow　　　　　B. fast　　　　　　C. racing　　　　　D. average

4. Driver _____ is a crucial factor in occupant protection because the most effective occupant protection device, the safety belt, works only when fastened.

　　A. performance　　B. training　　　　C. behavior　　　　D. studying

5. _____ is a major traffic safety problem in all countries in which alcohol is used widely, often accounting for about half of all fatalities.

　　A. Drunk driving　　B. Driver performance　　C. Driver behavior　　D. Racing-car driving

III. Translate the following sentences into Chinese.

1. The total is expected to increase steeply as the number of motor vehicles increases rapidly in many formerly less-motorized countries, and will likely exceed 2 million by the year 2020.

2. Injuries due to traffic crashes vastly outnumber fatalities, with over 5 million occurring per year in the US, most of them minor.

3. Research indicates that the risk of crashing increases approximately in proportion to travel speed, injury risk in proportion to travel speed squared, and fatality risk in proportion to travel speed to the fourth power.

4. A comparison of the gender and age dependence of involvement rates in severe single-vehicle crashes and in crimes unrelated to traffic offenses (say, burglary, as a typical example) show remarkable similarities.

5. The US study found the road user to be the sole factor in 57% of crashes, the roadway in 3%, and the vehicle in 2%; the corresponding values from the British study were 65%, 2% and 2% respectively.

IV. Discussions.

1. What are the factors that most affect road traffic fatality risk?

2. What is the difference between driver performance and drive behavior?

Reading Material: Measures to Improve Traffic Safety

For over a century measures have been introduced in many countries aimed at reducing harm from traffic crashes. There is extensive world experience, many failures, and many successes. In this section we address the relative contributions of different countermeasures.

Traffic fatalities have sometimes been discussed as being comparable to some single disease. I consider such an analogy unhelpful because it tends to suggest that the problem might be solved by the type of elegant knockout blow that conquered smallpox or scurvy. Any such hope tends to divert attention and resources from potentially effective realistic approaches to unrealistic approaches. A more appropriate and fruitful analogy is to health in general, with traffic safety and public health having the same broad goal of reducing death and morbidity. One of the simplest measures of overall health in a nation is average longevity, which has been increasing in nearly all industrialized countries. Longevity is strongly related to national wealth, measured by variables such as gross domestic product per capita. However, people in richer countries live longer for reasons that are more complex than the mere ability to purchase better medical care, important though this is. A country's traffic fatality rate (deaths per vehicle) is also strongly related to its wealth. However, some countries with similar wealth have important differences in longevity, and in traffic fatality rates. Those with the greatest longevity tend also to have the safest traffic.

It is universally accepted that many factors have made major contributions to increasing longevity. Some are technological in nature—surgery, antibiotics, vaccines, organ transplants, and the like. Some involve improved physical and institutional infrastructure such as better housing, sewage, ambulance service, and refrigeration. Some are legislative, such as laws regulating food and air quality, building inspection, and worker safety. Some come from changes in collective human behavior in hygiene, diet, exercise, sexual behavior, and use of alcohol and tobacco. Traffic fatality rate declines reflect contributions from these same broad categories—technology, infrastructure, legislation, and behavior change.

Large changes in longevity in time and between countries have close parallels in traffic fatalities. Data showed that the number of traffic fatalities for the same distance of travel in the US declined by 94% from 1921 to 2002, and the number of traffic fatalities per thousand vehicles declined by 96% from 1900 to 2002. In both cases the comparison is between the earliest and latest data, and the declines were reasonably constant at about 3% per year over each entire period. The number of traffic fatalities per thousand vehicles in some countries is 99% lower than in others during the same year. Understanding the origins of such large variations in time, and between countries, would be a step towards identifying the factors that contribute most to traffic safety.

The large number of factors relevant to traffic safety can be conveniently placed into broad categories. Weather is not part of the main structure because there is not much that can be done to change it, and, unlike the other factors, it remains relatively constant over the decades. Improved medicine plays an important role in reducing harm from traffic crashes in all categories, but its more detailed role is outside the scope of this book. If a patient arrives alive at a modern trauma center, survival chances are high. However, Fatality Analysis Reporting System (FARS) 2002 data show that 55% of those killed in traffic crashes died within an hour of their crashes. Recall that a typical fatality involves a single-vehicle crash at 2:00 am in a rural area, so that elapsed time from crash to arrival at a hospital is quite different than for daytime urban crashes.

The variation by a factor of more than a hundred in traffic fatalities per thousand vehicles between different countries cannot be due primarily to differences in vehicle engineering. While the mix of vehicles is certainly different in different countries, the vehicles in the high-rate (high values of fatalities per thousand vehicles) countries are essentially the same as in the low-rate countries, because the high-rate countries rarely manufacture vehicles, but instead import them from low-rate countries. In the high-rate countries the vehicles are older, but this is of little consequence because many analyses of data from low-rate countries find no large relationships between fatality rates and vehicle age. More recent vehicles may have stricter safety standards, but these could make no more than a modest difference, whereas the lowest rates are more than 99% below the highest rates. Roads, congestion, and other factors are also clearly different in the different countries. But these differences cannot come close to explaining the large variations observed. The only plausible explanation is that drivers are behaving sufficiently differently in the high-rate countries to generate a major portion of the observed difference.

Chapter 7 Public Transportation

➔ Text A History of Public Transportation

Public transportation is a shared passenger transportation service which is available for use by the general public, as distinct from modes such as taxicab, car pooling or hired buses which are not shared by strangers without private arrangement. Public transport modes include buses, trolleybuses, trams and trains, rapid transit (metro/subways/undergrounds etc) and ferries. Public transport between cities is dominated by airlines, coaches, and intercity rail. High-speed rail networks are being developed in many parts of the world.

Most public transport runs to a scheduled timetable with the most frequent services running to a headway. Share taxi offers on-demand services in many parts of the world and some services will wait until the vehicle is full before it starts. Paratransit is sometimes used in areas of low-demand and for people who need a door-to-door service.

Urban public transport may be provided by one or more private transport operators or by a transit authority. Public transport services are usually funded by government subsidies and fares charged to each passenger. Services are normally regulated and possibly subsidized from local or national tax revenue. Fully subsidized, zero-fare (free) services operate in some towns and cities.

For historical and economic reasons, there are differences internationally regarding use and extent of public transport. While countries in Old World tend to have extensive and frequent systems serving their old and dense cities, many cities of the New World have more sprawl and much less comprehensive public transport.

Mode of Public Transportation

Airline

An airline provides scheduled service with aircraft between airports. Air travel has high up to very high speeds, but incurs large waiting time prior and after travel, and is therefore often only feasible over longer distances or in areas where lack of ground infrastructure makes other modes of transport impossible. Bush airlines work more similar to bus stops; an aircraft waits for passengers and takes off when the aircraft is full.

Each operator of a scheduled or charter flight uses an airline call sign when communicating with airports or air traffic control centers. Most of these call-signs are derived from the airline's trade name, but for reasons of history, marketing, or the need to reduce ambiguity in spoken English (so that pilots do not mistakenly make navigational decisions based on instructions issued to a different aircraft), some airlines and air forces use call-signs less obviously connected with their trading name. For example, British Airways uses a Speedbird call-sign, named after the logo of its predecessor, BOAC, while SkyEurope used Relax.

Bus and coach

Bus services use buses on conventional roads to carry numerous passengers on shorter journeys. Buses operate with low capacity (i.e. compared with trams or trains), and can operate on conventional roads, with relatively inexpensive bus stops to serve passengers. Therefore buses are commonly used in smaller cities and towns, in rural areas as well for shuttle services supplementing in large cities. Bus services play a major role in the provision of public transport. These services can take many forms, varying in distance covered and types of vehicle used, and can operate with fixed or flexible routes and schedules. Services may be operated by public or private companies, and be provided using bus fleets of various sizes.

Bus rapid transit is an ambiguous term used for buses operating on dedicated right-of-way, much like a light rail. Trolleybuses are electric buses that employ overhead wires to get power for traction. Online Electric Vehicles are buses that run on a conventional battery, but are recharged frequently at certain points via underground wires.

Coach services use coaches (long-distance buses) for suburb-to-CBD or longer distance transportation. The vehicles are normally equipped with more comfortable seatings, a separate luggage compartment, video and possibly also a toilet. They have higher standards than city buses, but a limited stopping pattern. Coach scheduled transport is a mode of public transport by motor coach which is used in many countries around the world for longer distance journeys. Coaches are popular in countries which have no trains as the main form of long-distance transport or as a more flexible or cheaper alternative.

Train

A train is a connected series of rail vehicles that move along the track. Propulsion for the train is provided by a separate locomotive or from individual motors in self-propelled multiple units. Most trains carry a revenue load, although non-revenue cars exist for the railway's own use, such as for maintenance-of-way purposes. The engine driver controls the locomotive or other power cars, although people movers and some rapid transits are driverless.

Passenger rail transport is the conveyance of passengers by means of wheeled vehicles specially designed to run on railways. Trains allow high capacity on short or long distance, but require track, signalling, infrastructure and stations to be built and maintained. Urban rail transit consists of trams, light rail, rapid transit, people movers, commuter rail, monorail suspension railways and funiculars.

Ferry

A ferry is a boat or ship, used to carry (or ferry) passengers, and sometimes their vehicles, across a body of water. Most ferries operate on regular, frequent, return services. A foot-passenger ferry with many stops is sometimes called a water bus or water taxi. Ferries form a part of the public transport systems of many waterside cities and islands, allowing direct transit between points at a capital cost much lower than bridges or tunnels, though at a lower speed. Ship connections of much larger distances (such as over long distances in water bodies like the Mediterranean Sea) may also be called ferry services.

Text B Dial-A-Ride

Definition and Service Patterns

Service terms are basically synonymous with dial-a-ride: dial-a-bus, demand-responsive transit, and demand-actuated transit. All describe a type of service that is more flexible than conventional transit service. Service can be demand-responsive in two ways: (1) routing—the vehicle goes exactly where the passenger wants (door-to-door service)—and (2) scheduling—the vehicle arrives when desired by the passenger. Of course, taxis provide exactly these kinds of service. Most people reserve the term dial-a-ride for systems in which passengers going to different destinations may share the vehicle.

A dial-a-ride system has a defined service area rather than specific routes. It picks up and delivers riders within the service area, but does not go outside it. There are three service patterns:

(1) Many-to-one: Passengers are picked up anywhere but are delivered to only one place, such as a major employment site. This is usually paired with one-to-many service.

(2) Many-to-few: Passengers are taken to only a few places, such as downtown, a shopping center, and a hospital. This would be paired with one-to-many service.

(3) Many-to-many: Origins and destinations may be anywhere in the service area.

Some operations vary the service patterns depending on the time of day. For example, in the morning peak period, passengers are only taken to a railroad station, and in the evening peak, they are only picked up at the station. During the rest of the day, many-to-many service is offered.

Some systems attempt to fill requests that are telephoned to a dispatcher as soon as possible, but some wait time is inevitable. Many systems require that reservations be made in advance, often the previous day. Most will provide service on a regular, subscription basis. For example, a person might be picked up every morning at the same time to go to work or every Thursday to go to supermarket.

Dial-a-ride is intended for situations where the demand is too low for conventional transit service. These may be low-density areas such as suburbs, small cities and towns that have no scheduled bus service, or rural areas. Sometimes automobile ownership levels are high in these areas, but there are some people without cars. Another approach is to offer dial-a-ride service during evening and weekend hours as a substitute for scheduled bus service that operates in the daytime Monday through Friday.

The Vehicles

Most dial-a-ride services do not use the standard transit bus, which has at least 45 seats and costs from $175,000 upward. Instead they use smaller vehicles of four types:

(1) A standard van, which has 5 to 15 seats and costs $12,000 to $18,000 (prices are given as of 1988). This vehicle has the advantage that it can be purchased off the shelf, but it has a short service life (3 to 5 years) and its low roof makes getting in and out awkward.

(2) A modified van, which usually has a higher roof and sometimes a lower floor and wider body. It has 9 to 16 seats and costs $22,000 to $25,000. It can be equipped with a wheelchair lift. The disadvantages are that it gets poor fuel mileage and that a raised roof makes it unstable in high winds. See Figure 7.1.

Figure 7.1　A Typical Paratransit Vehicle

This modified van carries ten passengers and is equipped with a wheelchair lift at the rear. It provides demand-responsive service to senior citizens in Lawrence, Kansas.

(3) A body-on-chassis vehicle, of which the best-known example is the standard school bus. This is made by putting a bus on top of a chassis designed for a van, light-duty truck, or motor home. It has 12 to 30 seats and costs $35,000 to $45,000. It is more durable than vans, with a service life of 5 to 7 years, and has no significant disadvantages.

(4) A small bus. This is designed like a standard bus, with the same chassis and diesel engine, but with smaller dimensions. Typically there are 18 to 35 seats. This is very durable vehicle, with a service life of 10 to 15 years, and it has more interior space than the other types. The principal disadvantage is its price, which ranges from $100,000 to $120,000.

These vehicles have many other applications than dial-a-ride. One can normally observe a variety of all four types circulating at any major airport to carry travelers to hotels, car-rental agencies, parking lots, etc.

Vocabulary and Glossary

1. coach *n.* 长途客运
2. ferry *n.* 渡轮
3. funiculars *n.* 索道缆车
4. infrastructure *n.* 基础设施
5. monorail *n.* 单轨铁路
6. paratransit *n.* 辅助客运系统
7. subsidy *n.* 补贴;津贴;补助金
8. Timetable *n.* 时刻表
9. airline call sign 航空呼号
10. commuter rail 通勤火车
11. mass transit system 大众交通;公共交通
12. Public transportation 公共交通;大众交通
13. revenue load 收入客座率
14. sustainable transport 可持续交通

Exercises

I. True or false.

1. Paratransit is sometimes used in areas of low-demand and for people who need a door-to-door service. (   )

2. An aircraft doesn't wait for passengers and takes off when the aircraft is full. (   )

3. An aircraft doesn't wait for passengers and takes off on time. (   )

4. Bus services may be operated by public or private companies, and be provided using bus fleets of various sizes. (   )

5. A public transport timetable is provided in printed form, for example as a leaflet or poster. (   )

II. Translate the following sentences into Chinese.

1. Share taxi offers on-demand services in many parts of the world and some services will wait until the vehicle is full before it starts.

2. For historical and economic reasons, there are differences internationally regarding use and extent of public transport.

3. These services can take many forms, varying in distance covered and types of vehicle used, and can operate with fixed or flexible routes and schedules.

4. Coaches are popular in countries which have no trains as main form of long-distance transport or as a more flexible or cheaper alternative.

5. Ferries form a part of the public transport systems of many waterside cities and islands, allowing direct transit between points at a capital cost much lower than bridges or tunnels, though at a lower speed.

6. Typically, the timetable will list the times when the vehicle is scheduled to arrive at and depart from the specified locations.

III. Discussions.

1. How many ways do public transport modes include?

2. How to accept propulsion for a train?

3. Investments in infrastructure are high, and make up a substantial part of the total costs in systems that are expanding.

4. What are the main sources of financing for public transport?

5. Please talk about what is sustainable transport (or green transport).

Reading Material: Carpooling

Carpooling is an obvious way to take vehicle off the road. The average number of persons per car for all kinds of urban trips is about 1.5. It is lower for trips to work which is apparently about 1.1, despite the popular belief that car pools are common. Furthermore, car pools are becoming less common. According to the census, of those persons who used private vehicles to go to work, 23.5 percent carpooled in 1980, but only 15.4 percent in 1990. The number of persons who carpooled decreased by 4 million in the decade.

There are many empty seats in cars, which adds up to a lot of unused capacity. This is wasteful, but it also represents a reserve that is available for emergencies. For example, if another energy crisis and gasoline shortage occurred, carpooling would be the major response, unless the crisis went on for some time. Carpooling increases quickly and spontaneously in brief emergencies such as a transit strike or serve weather.

The author was working as a transportation planner in New York City at the time of the transit strike in 1966. One morning he was stationed on the Queensborough Bridge to count the number of persons in every automobile entering Manhattan. Over a 4-hour period, the average was 3.23 persons per automobile. The driver was alone in only 16 percent of the cars, while 44 percent of cars carried 4 or more persons.

However, as a habitual practice in normal times, carpooling is unpopular with most commuters. There are several reasons:

(1) Scheduling and routing are usually rigid. You can't work late or make a side trip on the way home if you are in a car pool.

(2) The dispersion of homes and workplace, especially in low-density areas, reduces the probability of finding good matches. Car pools work best with large employers where many people work in the same location.

(3) People who ride with someone else don't have a car available to run errands during the day or to go to lunch. Again, the dispersed character of suburban development often makes a car essential for such purposes. Many office and industrial parks have no eating places within walking distance.

(4) Personality conflicts make car pools unattractive to some. The majority of car pools do not have long tenure. People who have had bad experiences may not want to try again.

Teal made an analysis of carpooling with data from the 1977-1978 Nationwide Personal Transportation Survey. He found that carpoolers do not form a homogeneous group; they have a wide range of characteristics. About 40 percent of car pools contain members of the same household. Most of these are two-person car pools with a wife and husband. About 20 percent of carpoolers do not have any vehicle available and are always passengers.

Teal concluded that "economics plays a major role in carpooling. The commuters most prone to carpool are those making long trips, those with relatively high commuting cost burdens if they drive alone, and those from households with fewer vehicles than workers". But in his study, economic variables were not very successful in predicting car pool use.

Owens analyzed interview data in an attempt to find out why some people remained in car pools while others dropped out. Attitudinal factors were very important. Durable car pools had members who liked each other and felt that the arrangement was fair. Of course, such factors are not ascertained by computer matching programs.

Car pools depend on individual initiative; there is dispersed decision making in this situation. However, the government or other authorities can do things to increase carpooling, such as:

(1) Provide a matching service to pair people with the same general origin, destination, and time schedules. Matching can be done manually or by computer. It can be done for major employers or for the general public (some radio stations help promote it). This is basically an information service that can be offered, but people cannot be forced to use it. Evidence shows that only a small percentage of people given matches actually form car pools.

(2) Give car pools the most convenient spaces in parking lots. This is a common practice, but if the car pool spaces go unused, there may be a backlash.

(3) Arrange a guaranteed ride home program. People who occasionally must leave work at odd time, missing their car pools, can take a subsidized taxi ride home. In a demonstration in the Seattle area, 260 persons signed up, some of whom stopped driving alone. Each person was allowed a certain number of taxi miles per month, but had to pay $1 for each trip. The program, which cost the local government $8000 over 6 months, was deemed successful and was expanded.

(4) Install high-occupancy vehicle (HOV) lanes. This was done in many places around the country. What started as exclusive bus lanes have generally become HOV lanes. There is a prob-

lem with cheating unless police make a concerted enforcement effort. There have been cases in which drivers carried dummies in their cars. The driver of a hearse in Los Angeles was ticketed for using an HOV lane; the police did not accept his argument that the body in the coffin counted as a passenger.

HOV lanes have given rise to a new phenomenon called casual carpooling or instant carpooling, in which drivers pick up hitchhikers in order to use the lanes. Commuters find a place where they can park their cars free all day, and then they wait for a ride at standard pickup points. According to Beroldo, every weekday morning about 8000 commuters form casual car pools in the East Bay to cross the Bay Bridge to San Francisco. Automobiles with 3 or more persons may use a bypass lane at the toll plaza; which saves 10 to 20 minutes in travel time and lowers the toll by $1.

There are some remarkable things about this behavior. Some commuters from Contra Costa Country actually start on BART and get off to form a car pool to cross the bridge. There is a no bypass in the evening because tolls are collected only in the westbound direction. Hence the carpoolers find another way to get home. Indeed, BART carries about 5000 more passengers eastbound in the evening than westbound in the morning.

This custom seems like a logical way to remove cars from highways. However, Beroldo made a survey which showed that only 6 percent of the car pool passengers formerly drove alone, while 33 percent of the car pool drivers formerly used transit. Apparently the number of automobile using the Bay Bridge has increased.

The other place which happens on a larger scale is in Springfield, Virginia, where about 2500 persons a day form ad hoc car pools to use the HOV lanes on the Shirley Highway leading to Washington, D. C.. The transit authority first objected to the practice on the grounds that is unfair competition. Later the authority adjusted its service and was able to reduce operating costs. Reno et al. urged that this system be replicated elsewhere.

Planners often promote carpooling with the idea that it will reduce drive-alone commuting. However, Teal said that data indicates that it is transit use and carpooling that are close substitutes. In other words, greater carpooling will take passengers off the transit system, rather than drivers off the road. Teal found that carpooling is high in areas where the transit service is poor and low, while the carpooling is low in areas where transit service is good. He was pessimistic about efforts to increase carpooling significantly, but the record shows that it does happen when driving becomes difficult or expensive.

Chapter 8   Intelligent Transportation System

➡ Text A   Advanced Traveler Information Systems

What are advanced traveler information systems?

Advanced traveler information systems (ATIS) are an integral component of intelligent transportation systems (ITS). ATIS can provide transportation system users with more transportation options and higher travel efficiency. A person traveling to work, shop, or on a long-distance trip may want to know the best path to take in terms of distance, road or weather conditions, or places of interests along the way. Intermodal trips are facilitated when bus and train schedule and fare information is readily available. Prior knowledge of roadway congestion, incidents, and transit delays can reduce stress even if they cannot be entirely avoided. For consumer vehicle operators, such as truck and taxi drivers, traveler information can have direct impact on productivity and profitability, as it helps them avoid costly delays.

Traveler information can be provided before or during a trip. Pre-trip information provides a way to plan a path, the model of travel, and identify stops along the way. Because travel conditions can change once a trip has started, the ability to access traveler information during the course of the journey (en-route information) will be useful.

What distinguishes an ATIS from the low-tech approaches used to inform travelers in the past is how data are collected, processed, and delivered. In an advanced system, information is stored electronically in computer databases so it can be retrieved and delivered to the traveler when and where it is needed. Data are collected from sources as diverse as traffic and transit management systems, weather services, Yellow Pages, and tourist organizations. Telecommunications, including voice, data, or video transmissions over wireline or wireless networks, are the means by which travelers access ATIS databases across the whole spectrum of rapidly expanding technologies, such as cellular phones, cable television, handheld computers, and in-vehicle devices. Many ATIS systems in place today are evolving from manual, labor-intensive operations with limited distribution to more highly automated processes that can serve travelers on demand.

The following table (Table 8.1) shows an extensive list of data of potential interest to the traveler. This information may originate from government agencies (e.g., departments of transportation [DOTs], transit operators) or from private sources (e.g., Yellow Pages).

Potential Content of ATIS Table 8.1

Static information-known in advance, change frequently	Planned construction and maintenance activities
	Special events, such as parades and sporting events
	Toll costs and payment options
	Transit fares, schedules, routes, and so forth
	Intermodal connections
	Commercial vehicle regulations, such as hazmat and height and weight restrictions
	Parking locations and costs
	Business listings, such as hotels and gas stations
	Tourist destinations
	Navigational instructions
Real-time information, which changes frequently	Road-way conditions, including congestion and incident information
	Alternate routes
	Road weather conditions, such as snow and fog
	Transit schedule adherence
	Parking lot space availability
	Travel time
	Identification of next stop on train or bus

What are the objectives of ATIS?

ATIS must provide information that satisfies the needs of multiple individuals and organizations. For travelers, which range from commuters, tourists, business travelers, and operator of commercial vehicles for local or long-distance purposes, ATIS translates to more efficient and less stressful travel. Knowing which routes are to be avoided because of traffic congestion, what bus and train routes are available, and what routes have truck weight and height restrictions are just some of the types of questions that travelers are looking forward to be answered with ATIS. Public transportation agencies view ATIS as a transportation management tool that can help meet transportation policy objectives, such as managing traffic congestion or increasing transit use. By providing information to the users of the transportation network, agencies hope to effect travel behavior in a way that will benefit the system as a whole. Businesses involved in ATIS deployments are seeking profitable revenue opportunities for their ATIS products and services.

The extent to which an ATIS can accommodate multiple objectives is an open question, but logic dictates that ATIS planners identify the most important objective before a regional ATIS is developed. For example, if a public agency disseminates information for free to travelers, it may undercut the potential for the private sector to find paying customers for traveler information services.

Similarly, an ATIS focusing on traffic congestion and incident reporting on major roads will be of limited value for travelers who wish to plan multimodal trip. Finding the appropriate balance to competing objectives is the challenge for ATIS developers.

Enabling Technologies

ATIS is the beneficiary of a number of technologies that have experienced rapid growth and evolution in recent years. Although transportation was not the driving force behind the development of these enabling technologies, they provide the foundation on which ATIS applications can be built. Important enabling technologies include the following:

- Information processing speed of computers—enormous advances in the power of integrated circuits along with reduction in cost and size have helped to fuel the proliferation of equipment available for businesses and consumers alike.
- Digitalization—all types of information (i.e., voice, data, and image) can be stored in digital form, enabling data to be transmitted, stored, and processed in a similar manner.
- Wireless communications—are exploding both technologically and in market demand. Digital cellular and PCS, two-way paging, FM-subcarrier, and other wireless services enable mobile information.
- Speech technology—examples of speech technology include voice recognition and synthesized speech. Voice-activated interface technologies are tools that enable a person to give the computer (or other appliance) a voice command, a key step toward hands-free human interfaces.
- Global positioning system (GPS)—the GPS constellation of 24 satellites provides location coordinates to GPS receivers, which can determine location to 30-100 meters accuracy using three satellite signals.
- Miniaturization—creates enormous opportunities to put things precisely where they are needed with minimal weight and size.

◆ Text B Electronic Toll and Vehicle Classification

There are many reasons for charging different tolls for different vehicles on a roadway or at a crossing. The most common reason is to relate the toll to some measure of the damage or deterioration the vehicle causes to the road. Because heavier vehicles have greater effects, they are charged higher. Other reasons often used are cultural or political. In one state, recreational vehicles are charged a lower toll than comparable trucks; and in another, buses pay less than cars. Sometimes, place of residence determines the toll, in part. Usually, the damage and deterioration reason is combined with one or more cultural or political reasons in the assignment of tolls.

With the variety of tolling approaches and long before the advent of electronic toll collection (ETC), several authorities established individual, formal toll tables that relate tolls to physical vehicle characteristics, vehicle usage, or other cultural or political factors. The tables often required human toll collectors to make intelligent and sometimes subtle distinctions when assigning and collecting tolls in a lane. Once established and in use for a period of time, the toll tables become fixed elements in the society and have the force of law and are similarly hard to change. When ETC systems are deployed, they usually must incorporate the toll tables extant; it is unusual for the toll tables to be changes at those times.

Vehicle weight is universally agreed to be a major determinant of the rate at which roadways deteriorate in use. However, weighing a vehicle requires it to come to a stop on a truck scale, or to be weighed while it is in motion. Weigh-in-motion devices (WIM) are relatively new, always expensive and are not used for routine toll collection purposes. Rather, over the years, the number of axles and the number of wheels on each axle have been used by most authorities as a reasonable accurate measure of weight.

Classification

The anticipated widespread use of ETC required that authorities formalize a vehicle classification formulation that would allow each authority to charge a correct toll each vehicle using common vehicle features that could be observed by instrumentation and computer processed without requiring human participation. A leader in establishing such a formulation has been the IAG (E-ZPass Interagency Group); and other authorities use their own, comparable formulations. The IAG recognized that some vehicle features are easy to reliably detect by instrumentation, but others are harder. They also recognized that nonvehicle, political, or cultural features on the vehicle characteristics that can be measured with devices and computer processing that may be either already field deployed or might be deployed in the foreseeable future.

Matching

When a patron enrolls in an ETC system, that person's vehicle(s) is(are) described to the toll collection authority, which in turn assigns a vehicle class to each vehicle and adds that class to the record containing the transponder identification. A file of all such records (which is often voluminous because it contains information for every transponder in the ETC system) is stored in each ETC-capable lane in the authority's entire roadway and/or crossing system. Subsequently, when a vehicle appears in a toll collection lane, and AVC (automated vehicle classification) system installed there will take measurements of the vehicle and using programmed instructions, and then it will convert these measurements into a vehicle class. In real time, the ETC system in the lane will read the transponder identification number, access the vehicle classification assigned to the transponder and compare it with the classification determined by the AVC. If they match, toll corresponding to the classification is inserted into the patron's records. If the classifications do not match, further action is needed because a mismatch may indicate misuse of the transponder (such as an attempt to use a transponder with a lower classification to pay a toll for a vehicle for which a higher toll is warranted).

Automated Vehicle Classification

Most toll systems employ some form of AVC in order to determine the vehicle class and corresponding toll. AVC is typically comprised of one or more devices employed in the lane to gather information on the passing vehicle. AVC systems are deployed on a facility-by-facility basis and cannot be characterized by a standard configuration. AVC systems are selected to meet the needs of each individual agency.

For manual toll collection, typically some form of axle counting device is used to record vehicle axles as a check on the classification inputs entered by a toll collector. For electronic toll lanes, especially those with no toll collection personnel, these additional vehicle characteristics need to be determined and recorded in an automated fashion with no manual intervention. Various advanced techniques, employing complex algorithms receiving data from optical, acoustic, or video devices, have been used individually and in combination to meet the needs of individual agencies.

Two important elements must be determined by the AVC system: vehicle separation and vehicle axles. Vehicle separation allows the system to "frame" transactions, ensuring that collected vehicle characteristics are related to a single vehicle or physically attached combination for determination of the corresponding toll. Vehicle axles remain one of the most common determinants of a toll.

Two common approaches for the determination of vehicle separation are inductive loops and optical sensors. Loops are cut into the roadway surface and detect inductance changes created in the magnetic field above the loop when a vehicle passes. Because loops sense an area of coverage, they can be satisfactorily employed in high-speed installations where vehicles are widely separated but are problematic for lower speed locations where vehicles are closed spaced. Micro-loop probes reduce the coverage areas, but they remain susceptible on low-speed installations. Optical sensor, using infrared technology not visible to the human eye, offer true point detection and are advantageous in slow speed locations.

There are numerous axle-counting devices available. The simplest forms are the pneumatic tube and piezo-electric sensor. While these can successfully count axles, neither have been able to sustain the wear and tear of the continuous stop-and-go toll lane environment. Inductive loops and logic algorithms have been used with limited success because they are unable to sense a point. The overhead infrared sensors can be used to infer number of axles (based on length and height of profile) and are also being developed for a "side-fire" application that may more readily be able to determine vehicle axles. Lastly, video technologies are also used for AVC.

Vocabulary and Glossary

1. acoustic *adj.* 听觉的;声学的;原声的;音响的
2. algorithm *n.* 运算法则;算法;计算程序

3. cellular *adj.* 细胞的;由细胞组成的;多孔的;蜂窝状

4. commuter *n.* (远距离)上下班往返的人;通勤

5. congestion *n.* 拥挤,堵车;阻塞

6. deliver *v.* 发表;递送;交付

7. digitalization *n.* 数字化

8. disseminate *v.* 散布,传播

9. facilitate *v.* 促进,助长;使容易;帮助

10. inductance *n.* 电感

11. infrared *adj.* 红外线的

12. integral *adj.* 完整的;积分的;必须的

13. intermodal *adj.* 联合运输的

14. magnetic *adj.* 有磁性的,有吸引力的;磁性的

15. miniaturization *n.* 小型化

16. navigational *adj.* 航行的,航海的

17. optical *adj.* 视觉的,视力的;眼睛的;光学的

18. proliferation *n.* 增殖,分芽繁殖;再育;增生

19. retrieve *v.* 取回;恢复;[计]检索;重新得到

20. spectrum *n.* [物理学]谱,光谱;辐射源,能谱;光谱相片;范围;系列,范围,幅度

21. synthesize *v.* 综合;人工合成;(通过化学手段或生物过程)合成;(音响)合成

22. telecommunication *n.* 电信

23. warrant *v.* 保证,担保;授权,批准

24. Global Positioning System (GPS) 全球定位系统

25. in motion 在开动中,在运转中

26. pneumatic tube 气动导管

27. piezo-electric sensor 压电传感器

28. speech technology 语音技术

29. wireless communications 无线通信

Exercises

I. True or false.

1. Prior knowledge of roadway congestion, incidents, and transit delays can reduce stress even if they cannot be entirely avoided. (　　)

2. ATIS planners identify the most important objective before a regional ATIS is developed. (　　)

3. In one state, trucks are charged a lower toll than comparable recreational vehicles; and in another, cars pay less than buses. (　　)

4. Vehicle weight is universally agreed to be a major determinant of the rate at which roadways deteriorate in use. ( )

5. If ETC and AVC match, toll corresponding to the classification is inserted into the patron's records. ( )

II. Choose the best word or phrase to complete each statement.

1. Intermodal trips are _____ when bus and train schedule and fare information is readily available.
 A. retreated   B. facilitated   C. helped   D. reversed

2. Finding the appropriate _____ to competing objectives is the challenge for ATIS developers.
 A. balance   B. services   C. revenue opportunities   D. deployments

3. The IAG recognized that some vehicle features are easy to reliably _____ by instrumentation, but others are harder.
 A. find   B. discover   C. catch   D. detect

4. For _____ toll collection, typically some form of axle counting device is used to record vehicle axles as a check on the classification inputs entered by a toll collector.
 A. electronic   B. automatic   C. manual   D. electric

5. _____ allows the system to "frame" transactions, ensuring that collected vehicle characteristics are related to a single vehicle or physically attached combination for determination of the corresponding toll.
 A. Inductive loops   B. Optical sensors   C. Vehicle separation   D. Vehicle axles

III. Translate the following sentences into Chinese.

1. Many ATIS systems in place today are evolving from manual, labor-intensive operations with limited distribution to more highly automated processes that can serve travelers on demand.

2. With the variety of tolling approaches and long before the advent of electronic toll collection (ETC), several authorities established individual, formal toll tables that relate tolls to physical vehicle characteristics, vehicle usage, or other cultural or political factors.

3. When a patron enrolls in an ETC system, that person's vehicle(s) is described to the toll collection authority, which in turn assigns a vehicle class to each vehicle and adds that class to the record containing the transponder identification.

4. Subsequently, when a vehicle appears in a toll collection lane, and AVC (automated vehicle classification) system installed there will take measurements of the vehicle and using programmed instructions, and then it will convert these measurements into a vehicle class.

5. Inductive loops and logic algorithms have been used with limited success because they are unable to sense a point.

IV. Discussions.

1. What distinguishes an ATIS from the low-tech approaches used to inform travelers?

2. According to text A, list some of the types of questions that travelers are looking to answer with ATIS.

Reading Material: Applying ITS Technologies to TDM

Transportation demand management (TDM) has been succinctly described as the art of influencing traveler behavior with the aim of reducing automobile travel demand, or redistributing this demand in space or in time. TDM measures include promotion of transit and ridesharing, flexible working arrangements (e. g., staggered work hours, flextime), traffic calming and driving restrictions and prohibitions. These measures may be implemented through laws and regulations, promotional programs, monetary and tax incentives, pricing policies, planning requirements, negotiated agreements with developers and employer trip reduction programs. Increasingly, ITS is being used to facilitate and enhance TDM.

ITS technology is enhancing the management of travel demand in several ways. The following section describes specific applications of ITS in: (1) real-time traveler information, (2) interactive on-line ridematching, (3) parking management, (4) dynamic pricing of highway capacity, and (5) transit operations.

Real-time Traveler Information

Perhaps the best-known applications of advanced communication technologies to TDM are electronic real-time traveler information systems. Traveler information systems provide commuters and other travelers with timely and accurate information about travel choices. This information can be received at home, at work, or en route via a range of communication media. Prior to departure, radio, television, telephone, and computers can provide timely information about travel conditions, enabling travelers to choose the best travel mode, route and time of departure. Information about accidents, traffic speeds along given routes, weather and road conditions and special events that might disrupt traffic can be used by travelers to modify their travel plans. Information about transit routes, schedules and parking availability at rail stations can help travelers decide whether public transit is an effective option.

Once travel begins, car radios, visual displays, and other more advanced communication devices can provide travelers with updates about traffic conditions, transit service, incidents, and parking availability at destination. Roadside dynamic message signs (DMS), such as electronic signboards, and highway advisory radio (HAR) can alert motorists to current weather and road conditions. Visual displays at bus stops and rail stations can inform waiting passengers about arrival time and destination of the next train or transit bus. Vehicle-based route navigation systems containing map display can guide motorists traveling in unfamiliar surroundings to their destinations. Real-time traffic flow data can alert motorists to traffic problems ahead and re-route them around accidents and congestion bottlenecks.

Interactive On-line Ridematching

Internal computer systems known as local areas networks (LAN) or the Intranet are used in large workplaces to facilitate employer ridesharing. Intranets enable employees to do their own carpool matching using computer bulletin boards accessible through desktop computers or through touch-screen kiosks located in company cafeterias and public lobbies. Employees can enter their names, telephone numbers and carpool preferences into the database, confident that this personal information will only be shared with fellow employees.

Parking Information and Guidance Systems

Parking management is another aspect of TDM that has benefited from advances in communication technology. Electronic parking information and guidance systems provide motorists with accurate, continuously updated information about occupancy status of parking facilities. This allows motorists to select the most convenient parking location in advance and it spares them the frustration of a time-consuming search for a parking space. Typically, motorists approaching their destination encounter a tier of variable message signs showing a continuously updated inventory of available parking spaces at various parking facilities. Parking information and guidance systems can be used to facilitate access to parking garages in central business districts, surface parking lots on the periphery of downtown areas, park-and-ride lots serving suburban commuter rail stations, satellite parking lots at airports and parking areas surrounding sports and entertainment complexes. Still relatively little is known in the United States. Electronic parking information and guidance systems are used extensively in the cities of Western Europe, where severe congestion and shortage of space in city centers provide a strong incentive for their deployment. Overseas experience suggests that parking information systems can serve as an effective TDM tool. They can help disperse parking demand, relieve downtown congestion, achieve more efficient use of existing parking facilities, and guide tourists and visitors who are unfamiliar with the area.

Dynamic Pricing of Highway Capacity

ITS technology has also enhanced the feasibility of dynamic pricing of road facilities. While the concept of peak period pricing has been applied in many sectors of the private economy for many years, the use of variable pricing to control demand for road space in order to maintain a given level of service has been stymied by the complexity of collecting variable-rate tolls (i.e., tolls that vary by the time of day or with the level of congestion). Now, ETC technology allows variable-rate tolls to be deducted from the drivers' pre-paid, stored-value tag while the vehicle is in motion. This cashless, remote toll collection capability has made it possible to control demand in real-time and maintain free-flowing traffic conditions on tolled facilities. This approach has found its first application on two highway facilities in California: the private built and operated SR91 Express Lanes in Orange County, California; and the I-15 high-occupancy and toll lanes north of San

Diego, California.

Transit Service Enhancements

Automatic vehicle location (AVL) systems (i.e., wireless technologies that track buses and report their position to a central control station in real-time) have been used by transit agencies to improve productivity and operating performance of their bus fleets for several years. Now, AVL systems are being applied to TDM by communicating bus schedule information to the public and allowing dynamic schedule of transit services. Electronic displays at bus stops in numerous European cities inform waiting passengers when the next bus will be along, thus eliminating a common source of rider dissatisfaction with public transit.

Part III
技巧篇

翻译技巧

➡ 技巧一：词类的转译

在英译汉过程中,有些句子可以逐词对译,有些句子则由于英汉两种语言的表达方式不同,就不能用"一个萝卜一个坑"的方式来逐词对译。在很多情况下,需要转换词类,才能使译文通顺自然。常见的词类转译法有名词、形容词、动词、副词和介词的转译。

一、名词的词类转译

(一) 名词译成动词

英语中具有动作意义的名词和由动词派生出来的名词以及某些表示身份特征或职业的名词(如 teacher、singer 等)在句中并不指身份或职业而含有较强的动作意味,英译汉时须译成动词。

The sight and sound of our jet planes filled me with special longing.
看到我们的喷汽式飞机,听见隆隆的机声,令我特别神往。

The next news bulletin, shorter than usual, made no mention of the demonstration.
下一个新闻节目比通常短,没有提到游行。

The operation of a machine needs some knowledge of its performance.
操作机器需要懂得机器的一些性能。

(二) 名词译成形容词

由形容词派生出来的名词,翻译时译成形容词。例如：

Independent thinking is an absolute necessity in study.
独立思考对学习是绝对必需的。

The security and warmth of the destroyer's sickbay were wonderful.
驱逐舰的病室很安全也很温暖,好极了。

(三) 名词译成副词

当表达心情、感觉的名词后接动词词组,翻译时名词译成副词。例如：

It is our great pleasure to note that China has made great progress in economy.
我们很高兴地看到,中国的经济已经有了很大的发展。

二、形容词的词类转译

(一) 形容词译成动词

英语中表示知觉、欲望等心理状态的形容词,在联系动词后作表语时,往往可译成动词。

Scientists are confident that all matter is indestructible.

科学家们深信,所有物质都是不灭的。

Granny Li is very fond of children.

李奶奶很喜欢孩子。

(二) 形容词译成名词

He was eloquent and elegant-but soft.

他有口才、有风度,但很软弱。

(三) 形容词译成副词

当英语名词转译成动词时,修饰该名词的形容词往往转译成相应的副词。例如:

He then acted as a reluctant interpreter.

他当时并非情愿地当了一次翻译。

They regarded him as a potential adversary.

他们认为他可能是他们的一个对头。

三、动词的词类转译

动词译成名词(一般是名词派生的动词或名词转用的动词)

To them, he personified absolute power.

在他们看来,他就是绝对权威的化身。

Neutrons act differently from protons.

中子的作用不同于质子。

四、副词的词类转译

(一) 副词译成动词

She opened the window to let fresh air in.

她把窗子打开,让新鲜空气进来。

Now, I must be away, the time is up.

现在我该离开了,时间已经到了。

(二) 副词译成形容词

The film impressed me deeply.

这部电影给我留下了深刻的印象。

(三) 副词译成名词

They have not done so well ideologically, however, as organizationally.

但是,他们的思想工作没有他们的组织工作做得好。

五、介词的词类转译

介词译成动词

They went out after new mineral resources day by day.

他们天天外出寻找新矿源。

The president took the foreign guests around the campus.

校长带着外宾参观校园。

由此看来，英译汉时我们应该重视词类的转换以使译文通顺、自然，符合汉语的表达习惯。

●技巧二：被动句的译法

英汉两种语言，都有被动结构。然而，英语有别于汉语的特点之一，正在于被动语态的广泛应用，而汉语中较少使用被动语态。

两者有别的另一个特点是被动语态的构成各异。英语是"形合"语言，其被动语态是通过改变动词的形式来实现的，汉语是"意合"语言，其被动语态则由有明表被动之意或靠暗含被动之义的字词来实现的。

英语被动语态的广泛应用，自有其道理。在说不出主动者或不愿意说出主动者，或没有必要说出主动者或为了突出被动者，或为使上下文连贯衔接时，使用被动语态就方便多了。而且，被动语态把要说明的问题放在句子的主语位置上，既更能唤起人们的注意，又不带感情色彩，简洁客观。这些独特之处，尤其适应科技作品的需要。

汉语被动语态的使用范围较窄，是因为汉语突出主题，而英语突出主语，汉语具有英语所没有的无主句，许多被动句可以用无主句来代替。

然而，英语的被动结构，也不能滥用。在新闻写作上，美国名记者、语言大帅杰克·卡彭就在《美联社新闻写作指南》上提出"避免讨厌的被动语态"，"只要有可能就应当使用主动语态"。他认为，"在多数情况下，被动语态是松弛无力的，它把采取行动的人排除在画面之外。这是为什么官样文章的作者都醉心于被动语态的原因。"

他举例说，Police arrested John Smith（警察逮捕了约翰·史密斯）要比 John Smith was arrested by police（约翰·史密斯被警察逮捕）更为简洁、利落、有力。当然，如果约翰·史密斯是一位公众人物，为了新闻价值的要求，他的大名可以打头。

他还讲了一个饶有趣味的实例，说明软弱无力的被动语态和坚定有力的主动语态的区别是实际的而且带有预兆的性质。在敲诈勒索和恐怖威胁的信件中说"我要杀了你"的人，可能是真会玩命的，而说"你会被杀死"的人则有可能动摇，不敢"公然承认自己就是发出威胁的人"。

了解两种语言在被动语态中的异同以及英语被动语态的应用特点，可以帮助人们准确把握被动结构的句子，获得理想的译文。

被动结构的翻译方法，主要有如下几种：

一、化"被动"为"主动"

一般来说,由于英语被动语态结构用得多,英译汉时,变为主动语态的情形也就十分普遍了。而这种化"被动"为"主动"的技巧,在实际操作上,也是多种多样的。

(一)译为有主句

这里,又有"反宾为主,变主为宾"、"增译主语,泛指'有人'"和"原文主语,'主'位坐稳"三种情形:

1. 反宾为主,变主为宾

翻译时,把原文的主语,即行为的客体,译成宾语而把主体或相当于行为主体的介词宾语译成主语。这里举一个有趣的例子:

【例1】

The times is read by the people who run the country; The Guardian is read by the people who would like to run the country; The Financial Times is read by the people who own the country and The Daily Telegraph is read by the people who remember the country as it used to be.

这是一段说明报纸读者群体情况的英文原文。不同的报纸,拥有不同的读者,不同的读者追逐不同的消息。因此,就有了下面四句意味深长的打油诗:

在位掌权的人读《泰晤士报》,渴望掌权的人读《卫报》,大老板们读《金融时报》,怀念大英帝国曾经了不起的人读《每日电讯报》。

【例2】

Modern scientists have discovered that energy may be created from matter and that matter, in turn, may be created from energy.

现代科学家发现:物质可以产生能,能可以产生物质。

2. 增译主语,泛指"有人"

翻译时,把原文的主语译成宾语,增译"有人"、"人们"、"大家"、"我们"等泛指性的主语。

【例3】

With the rapid development of modern science and technology, information can be sent to every part of the world.

随着现代科学技术的迅速发展,我们能把各种各样的信息传到世界各地。

【例4】

To explore the Moon's surface, rockets, satellites and airships were launched again and again.

为了探测月球的表面,人们一次又一次地发射火箭、卫星和飞船。

3. 原文主语、"主"位坐稳

翻译时,原文的主语地位不变,在译文中仍为主语。这时,汉语译文中虽无"被"字,但被动的意义已暗合在内。

【例5】

Over the last 20 years, the traffic theories have been developed to fit the observed data.

在过去的20年中,交通理论已经发展到可以符合观测的数据。

【例6】
New high-tech achievements have been applied to agricultural production.
高新科技的成果已应用于农业生产。

【例7】
If the technology and techniques are really advanced, co-operation can be prolonged.
如果技术确实先进,合作期限可以延长。

在不知道或者不必说出行为主体时,常常可以发挥汉语译文的优势,把英语的被动语态译成汉语的无主句。这时,原文的主语译为动词的宾语。

【例8】
Before any road work is carried out, the traffic engineer should be informed so that a programme of work can be agreed.
在任何道路开展工作之前,应该通知交通工程师,以便就工作程序达成一致。

(二)主语谓语合译

英语的一些动词成语含有名词,如 make use of, pan attention to, take care of, make reference to, take account of 等,变成被动语态时成了名词作主语的特殊被动语态。汉译时,可以把主语和谓语合起来翻译,译成汉语无主句的谓语。

【例9】
Care should be taken at all times to protect the computers and other instruments in the lab from dust and damp.
要始终注意保护实验室中的电脑和其他仪器,勿使其沾上灰尘,勿使其受潮。

【例10】
Use can be made of these materials to write a report on the delegation's visit to South Africa.
可以利用这些资料写一份该代表团访问南非的报告。

二、以"主动"表"被动"

汉语有一种"是……的"结构,是一种形式主动,实际上是不用"被"字的被动句,着重说明一件事情是如何产生或在何时何地产生的。在翻译英语被动结构时,可以利用这种形式主动的"是……的"结构,表示被动的实际意义。

【例11】
These stone processing machines have been introduced from Italy for the newly established factory.
这些石材加工机器是为新建工厂从意大利引进的。

【例12】
The secondary school is named after a donator who made a contribution of 50 million RMB yuan.
这所中学是以一名出资5000万元人民币的捐赠人的名字命名的。

【例13】
Although the dreams of seeing and hearing things from far, far away was made by human beings several thousand years ago, such dreams came into reality in modern times.

虽然"千里眼"和"顺风耳"是人类几千年前所梦想的但直到现代社会才梦想成真。

【例14】

This five star hotel was built in 1997 for Hong Kong's return to the motherland.

这家五星级酒店是为迎接香港回归祖国而于1997年建成的。

三、以"被动"译"被动"

虽然汉语被动语态使用的范围较窄,但并不是说汉语极少用被动句。有人认为汉语有四种表示被动的方式:

(1)在谓语前加上"被"字;

(2)在行为主体前加上"被"、"由"、"受"、"为……所"等字;

(3)谓语前省去"被"字不出现行为主体的被动句;

(4)"是……的"的结构。前面已把第三种方式归入"化'被动'为'主动'",把第四种方式列为"以'主动'表'被动'",因此,这里只谈谈前面两种方式。

(一)谓语之前加"被"字

当英语被动结构的句子中没有出现行为主体时,汉译句子可以在谓语的前面加上"被"字,表示原文的被动意义。

【例15】

Much of the energy is absorbed as the Sun's rays pass through the atmosphere.

太阳光线通过大气层时许多能量被吸收去了。

【例16】

Imagine that one or other continent is left out, forgotten, reduced to its poverty and its disorder; what will happen to the others?

想象一下,假如这块或那块大陆被遗漏或忘记,变得贫困混乱,其他大陆将会发生什么情况呢?

(二)行为主体前加"把"、"被"、"由"等字

在英语被动结构的句子中出现行为主体时,译文可使用汉语表示被动的语言手段,在其前面加上"把"、"被"、"由"、"受"、"遭"、"给"、"为……所"等字来突显原文句中的被动意义。

【例17】

I am now writing you, on behalf of the city delegation, to express our appreciation for the hospitality which was accorded to us during our visit to your city.

我现在代表本市代表团给您写信,对我们在贵市访问期间受到的热情款待表示感谢。

【例18】

The proposal on the improvement of the investment environment is accepted by all the members of the committee.

这条关于改善投资环境的建设为该委员会全体委员所接受。

【例19】

Some achievements in scientific research are limited by their cost in practical use.

一些科研成果的实际应用受到了成本问题的限制。

【例20】

The Moon, the stars and the Sun are made use of by the seamen to find their latitude and longitude at sea.

月亮、星星和太阳常被海员们用来确定海上的经纬度。

【例21】

Jimmy felt uneasy for the whole day as he was aroused from deep sleep by the ringing of the door bell early in the morning.

一大清早的大门铃声把吉米从沉睡中吵醒后,他整天都无精打采。

四、打破原结构,译成新句型

语言是变化多样的,英语被动结构的句子的译法灵活多样,无定规可寻,无一成不变的格式可套,就连被动语态的原来结构也可以打破,译成新的其他句型。

【例22】

The conflict was intensified by the different way in which the countries set out after they achieved independence between the two World Wars.

这一矛盾由于这些国家在两次世界大战中间取得独立后起步的路子不同而加深了。

【例23】

This co-operation is rendered without calculation, without ulterior motive and without mercantile interest.

进行合作时没有其他考虑,没有不可告人的用心,也不唯利是图。

【例24】

"Not to be served, but to serve"

这是香港中华基督教青年会郭琳褒纪念堂奠基石上的刻字。原文简洁典雅,石上的中文亦古朴简练,仅用八个汉字对译七个英文单词:"非以役人,乃役于人"。

五、常见形式主语被动句型的翻译

英语有不少被动句子,以 it 为形式主语、即"it + be + that"结构,汉译时通常使用主动语态,有时不加主语,有时加上泛指性主语,如"有人"、"大家"、"人们"、"众"等。

不加主语的:

It is found that... 据发现……

It is said that... 据说……

It is hoped that... 希望……

It is reported that... 据报道……

It may be safely said that... 可以有把握地说……

It has been illustrated that... 据(图示)说明……

It has been viewed that... 已经讨论了

It was first intended that... 最初就有这样的想法……

It is enumerated that... 列举了……
It is weighted that... 权衡了……
It may be said without fear of exaggeration that... 可以毫不夸张地说……
It must be pointed out that... 必须承认……
可加主语的：
It is well known that... 众所周知……
It is taken that... 有人认为……
It is noted that... 人们注意到……

技巧三：省译与增译

一、省译法

（一）冠词的省译
1. 不定冠词的省译
（1）不定冠词表示类别时的省译：
【例1】
An action plan is a formal document describing organization and procedures to be followed.
实施性规划是一个叙述应予遵循的有关组织和程序的正式文件。
（2）固定词组中不定冠词的省译：
【例2】
On a large scale 大规模地；with a view to 为了，以便；as a rule 通常。
注：不定冠词在某些情况下是不能省译的，如：不定冠词具有明显的数字概念。
【例3】
Sound is propagated as a pressure wave.
声音是以一种压力波的形式传播的。
不定冠词表示单位之意时，则常被译为"每"或"一"。
【例4】
A vehicle's limit speed in freeway is 80 kilometers an hour.
机动车在高速公路上的限速是80km/h。
（3）不定冠词出现在被修饰的名词前：
当一个名词作表语，并有一个表示特征的形容词修饰该名词时，这类名词前的不定冠词一般不省译。
【例5】
Carbon steel is an important material used on railway.
碳钢是一种应用于铁路的重要原材料。
2. 定冠词的省译
（1）定冠词表示类别时的省译：

【例6】

The plane is widely used in the world now.

现在飞机已在全世界广泛使用了。

(2)定冠词用于独一无二的对象时的省译:

【例7】

The plane is widely used in the world now.

现在飞机已在全世界广泛使用了。

(3)定冠词用于表示方位、左右等名词前的省译:

【例8】

The aerodrome is in the northwest of the city.

这个小型机场坐落于该市的西北角。

(4)定冠词与形容词、分词连用时的省译:

【例9】

The latter is more efficient.

后一类效率更高。

His work is to rescue the dying in a traffic accident.

他的工作是抢救那些在交通事故中濒临死亡的伤者。

(5)专有名词前定冠词的省译:

【例10】

the People's Republic of China 中华人民共和国;

the United States 美国;the Rocky Mountains 洛基山脉。

(6)定冠词在形容词最高级前的省译:

【例11】

The equipment is the most expensive one in my lab.

这套设备是我们实验室里最贵的。

(7)定冠词在"the + 比较级……,the + 比较级……"结构中的省译:

【例12】

The thinner the air is, the less support it gives to the plane.

空气越稀薄,给飞机的支撑力就越小。

(8)定冠词在固定词组中的省译:

【例13】

at the same time 同时;in the end 最后;for the time being 暂时。

注:定冠词在某些情况下必须译出,即当定冠词起着指示代词(this、that、these、those)的作用时,就被译为"这(该),那,这些或那些"。

【例14】

Please give me the experimental data.

请把那些实验数据给我。

(二)代词的省译

英语中代词可分为九种:人称代词、物主代词、自身代词、相互代词、指示代词、疑问代词、关系代词、连接代词和不定代词。其中不少代词在一定场合下都可省译。本书主要论述如下三种代词的省译。

1. 人称代词的省译

(1) 省译作主语的人称代词(常用于主语相同的并列句、复合句的其中一个主语的省译或主语泛指一般人的省译):

【例15】

The finished products should be sampled to check their quality before they leave the factory.

成品在出厂之前应该进行抽样质量检查。

Multiplying five by five, you get twenty-five.

5乘5得25。

(2) 第三人称代词作宾语时的省译(常用于前后关系清楚的句子):

【例16】

The vehicle emission is harmful to us and we should by all means remove them.

机动车排放物对我们是有害的我们应该尽量加以排除。

(3) it的省译(常用于it指代天气、距离、时间或某种状态的句子):

【例17】

It is eight sharp now.

现在是八点整。

2. 自身代词的省译

【例18】

We should concern ourselves here only with the traffic noise.

我们在此只论述交通噪声的问题。

3. 物主代词的省译(常用于物主代词较多的句子)

【例19】

He covered his face with his hand as if protect his eyes.

他用手蒙住脸,好像要去保护眼睛。

(三) 介词的省译

汉语中介词用得较少,词与词之间的关系往往是通过上下文表示出来的,因此汉译时介词常可省译。

1. 表示时间的介词的省译

【例20】

On May second the MRT construction was finished on May second.

五月二日,该地铁修建完成。

注:表示时间的介词译于句末时,该介词不能省译。

【例21】

The subway construction was finished on May second.

该地铁的修建完成于五月二日。

2. 表示地点的介词的省译

【例22】

The radio waves are very weak when they arrive at the television receiving sets on earth.

无线电波到达地面上的电视接收机时是相当微弱的。

注：表示地点的介词接于动词之后时，该介词不能省译。

【例23】

Mount the meter on that panel.

把仪表装在那块板上。

3. 用作状语或定语的介词短语中的介词的省译

【例24】

It is necessary to develop our railway at high speed.

必须高速发展我国铁路。

The products produced by our factory are good in quality and low in price.

我厂生产的产品物美价廉。

4. 用作补语的介词短语中的介词的省译（常用于谓语动词为 consider、find 等，且后面跟介词短语作补语的句子）

【例25】

In many caricatures a vehicle is usually pictured as a machine with pollution emission.

在很多讽刺漫画里机动车都被描画成吐着废气的机器。

（四）连词的省译

汉语中介词用得较少，语句的逻辑关系是靠词序或语序表示的，这就是汉语用意合法的特点，因此汉译时介词常可省译。

1. 并列连词的省译（最常见的是 and、or 和 but 的省译）

【例26】

The vehicular engine has worked in succession for seven or eight hours.

这辆车的发动机已经连续工作了七八个小时了。

2. 从属连词的省译

（1）时间状语从句中某些从属连词的省译：

【例27】

As traffic volume increased, the pollution from this source also increased.

交通量增加了，其产生的污染也便随之增加了。

（2）条件状语从句中某些从属连词的省译：

【例28】

If traffic volume increase, the pollution from this source also increase.

交通量增加，其产生的污染也增加。

（3）原因状语从句中某些从属连词的省译：

【例29】

Since transistors are extremely small in size and require only small amount of energy, they can make previously large equipment much smaller.

晶体管非常小,而且所需能量也少,它能时以前的大设备变得非常小。

(4) that 的省译:

【例 30】

The fact is that the experimental result is not obvious.

事实上,实验结果并不明显。

(五) 动词的省译

1. 某些系动词的省译

【例 31】

The research is on for a new clean fuel to serve this purpose.

该研究致力于寻找一种新型清洁燃料来实现这一目标。

2. 动词与具有动作意味的名词连用可省译

【例 32】

Then came the development of subway.

后来地铁发展起来了。

(六) 同位语的省译

当同位语是本位语(被其说明的词)的别名,在汉语中两者的译名又是相同的,则该同位语可省译。

【例 33】

In processing, or refining, petroleum, the several fractions are separated from each other.

在提炼石油的过程中,各种馏分彼此分开。

二、增补法

(一) 增补语义上、修辞上需要的词

1. 在某些名词、动名词前后增补动词

【例 34】

Testing is a complicated problem and long experience is required for this mastery.

进行测试是一个复杂的问题,需要有长期的经验才能掌握。

The molecules get closer and closer with the pressure.

随着压力增加,分子也越来越接近。

2. 增补一些附加性的词

【例 35】

Try to control your impatience during experiments when any unexpected problem arises.

当实验中出现没有预料到的问题时要尽量控制住你的急躁情绪。

3. 增补某些概括性的词

【例 36】

This report summed up the new research achievements made by the institute in subway and light rail.

这个报告总结了该研究院在地铁和轻轨两方面的研究成果。

4. 增补某些联系性的词

【例37】

Making experiments, we should carefully write down the results.

在做实验时,我们应当仔细地把结果记录下来。

5. 增补某些解释性的词

【例38】

While in your country he will be hoping to meet with all related parties for detailed discussion concerning ITS products.

在贵国逗留期间,他希望和有关各方都见见面,详细谈谈ITS产品业务。

6. 增补量词

【例39】

The landing gear of an airplane consists of three or more wheels.

飞机的起落架通常是由三个或更多的轮子组成的。

7. 增补表示复数含义的词

【例40】

The jet airplanes are flying over the sky.

一架架喷气式飞机正掠过天空。

注:大部分英语名词复数形式都带有-s或-es,但也有一些名词复数形式并无-s或-es,汉译时要视其需要译出复数含义。

【例41】

man→men 人;bacterium→bacteria 细菌;

Chinese→Chinese 中国人。

(二)增补原文中的省略部分

1. 增补回答部分的省略成分

【例42】

Is the vehicle's speed 80 km/h?

Yes, it is.

这辆机动车的速度是80km/h吗?

是的,它的速度是80km/h。

2. 增补并列句中的省略成分

【例43】

The route length of A is 100km, of B 120km.

A的路线长度为100km,而B的路线长度为120km。

3. 增补复合句中的省略成分

(1)增补比较状语从句中的省略成分:

【例44】

A is a little less dense than B.

A的密度比B的密度略小。

(2)增补主语:
【例45】
If being seen in the context of an overall urban transport strategy, public transport priority can provide an enhanced transport environment for the city.
如果公交优先被看作整个城市交通战略的一部分,就可为该市提供更好的交通环境。

(三)增补原文的内容语意
1. 关于形容词最高级的增补
【例46】
The strongest spring leads to fatigue failure caused by excessively high stress.
即使强度最大的弹簧,由于应力过大,也会导致疲劳损坏。

2. 关于 could…with 结构的增补
【例47】
The vehicular life could be significantly improved with the good use of its engine.
如果好好地使用发动机,机动车寿命就可显著延长。

3. 关于 with 引起的短语的增补
【例48】
With all his achievements he remains modest and prudent.
尽管他有很多成就,但他还是谦虚谨慎。

技巧四:长句的译法

在交通工程专业英语中最常见也最难理解的组成部分就是长句,它们由短句复合而成,常常是一个主句带若干个从句,从句带短语,短语带从句,从句套从句,互相依附,相互制约,因而使其显得错综复杂。在翻译长句时,需要运用综合分析法,具体应用如下:

一、弄清关系,分明主次,化整为零

在翻译长复合句时,首先要抓连接词(无连接词时抓谓语),将复合句划分为简单句其次分清主从关系;然后确定各简单句内的次要成分与主要成分的关系;最后将各简单句按逻辑进行串联,这样就有主有从,主次分明了。

【例1】
Although it may take some time to set up, we now have to install a communications infrastructure that will support computer-based wagon control and other management information systems that are bound to be installed in the future.
分析:这是一个比较简单的复合句,根据连接词 although 和两个 that,可知该句可分为部分,每 5 部分都是简单句:
(1) Although it may take some time to set up, we now have to install a communications infrastructure
(2) that will support computer-based wagon control and other management information sys-

tems

(3) that are bound to be installed in the future

第(1)句为 Although 引导的让步状语从句,(2)、(3)为定语从句,分别修饰 a communications infrastructure 和 other management information systems。因此,按全句的语法关系,结合上下文的含义,把各个简单句的译文串起来,从而可得到忠实通顺的译文。

参考译文:虽然建立通信网络需要时间,但是我们必须安装一套通信基础设施来支持以计算机为基础的车辆控制信息系统和其他将来必定要建立的管理信息系统的发展。

二、注意组合,看清前后搭配

出于修辞或句子结构安排的原因,英语中的固定词组在句子中有时会被隔开,这给翻译带来了困难。因此,凡遇到有些词前后关系不清时,就得考虑是否是被某个词组或短语隔开了。

【例2】

One method, used in the United States, to trace through a junction the paths of vehicles approaching along one leg only is to ask the motorist, through prominently displayed signs, to switch on the vehicle's headlights while going through the junction.

分析:固定词组 ask to 被插入语 through…signs 隔开了。

参考译文:用在美国的一种跟踪车辆通过交叉口路径的方法是当车辆到达交叉口的一条道路上,只要请驾驶人在通过交叉口时,遇到突出显示的指示牌的地方打开车灯。

三、注意分隔结构,搞清内在联系

英语句子的各种分裂结构是地道的英语特点之一,造成这种结构的原因是出于对修辞及句子结构的合理安排的考虑。在翻译这类句子时,应首先分析各成分之间的关系,搞清内在联系。

【例3】

The shield itself, slightly larger in diameter than the complete tunnel, encloses a circular steel cutting edge, which is forced slowly forward along the line of the tunnel.

分析:与主语关系密切的谓语 encloses 被 slightly larger…tunnel 这个独立结构隔开了。

参考译文:盾构本身直径略大于完工后的隧道直径,装在盾构内的一个钢制环形切削刃被推着沿隧道的走向缓缓前进。

➡技巧五:数字的译法

英语中表示数量的大小一般采用两种形式:一种是用阿拉伯数字表示;另一种是用文字表示。但是需要注意的是 1000 以上的数,若用阿拉伯数字表示,要先从个位数起,每三位数加一个分隔号",",第一个分隔号前为 thousand(千),第二个分隔号前为 million(百万),从第三个分隔号往前数,英国与美国的表示方法就有差异了。

milliard:英国为 10^9;

billion：英国为 10^{12}，美国为 10^9；
trillion：英国为 10^{18}，美国为 10^{12}；
quadrillion：英国为 10^{24}；
quintillion：英国为 10^{18}，美国为 10^{30}。
在翻译这些大数字时，应先分清原文是英国英语还是美国英语。

一、倍数增加的翻译法

（一）…n times ＋ 比较级 ＋ than…

表示净增的倍数，可照译为"n 倍"。

【例1】

Some electronic computers can do calculations 500,000 times faster than any person can.

有些电子计算机，其运算速度比人快 500 000 倍。

（二）…n times ＋ as…as

表示是……的 n 倍，也可译为"$n-1$ 倍"。

【例2】

Line A is twice as long as line B.

A 线的长度是 B 线的两倍。（或译为：A 线比 B 线长一倍。）

注：英语中，一倍用 once，两倍用 twice 或 double，三倍用 thrice 或 three times 表示；三倍以上的一概在基数词后面加 times 表示。

如果在 as…as 前不是倍数而是分数，则翻译方法如下：

【例3】

Wheel A turns one-tenth as fast as wheel B.

A 轮的转速是 B 轮的 1/10。（或译为：A 轮的转速比 B 轮慢 9/10。）

（三）…as much(many, fast) again as…

表示净增加一倍。

【例4】

The subway constructed this year is as long again as that old one.

今年新建的地铁比那条旧的长一倍。（或译为：今年新建的地铁是那条旧的两倍。）

注：如果在第一个 as 前加 half，则译为"一倍半于……"或"比……多（快）50%"。

【例5】

The subway constructed this year is half as long again as that old one.

今年新建的地铁比那条旧的长 50%。（或译为：今年新建的地铁是那条旧的一倍半。）

（四）…n times ＋ 名词或 that…

表示为……的 n 倍，也可译为"n 倍于……"。

【例6】

The volume of road A is about 4 times that of road B.

道路 A 的交通流量是道路 B 的 4 倍。

（五）表示增加意义的动词 ＋n times

表示增加了 $n-1$ 倍。

【例7】

The volume of the city has increased 5 times as again 1995.

该市的交通流比1995年增长4倍。(或译为:该市的交通流增长到1995年的5倍。)

(六)表示增加意义的动词 + by n times

表示净增的数,可照译为"增加 n 倍"。

【例8】

The abrasive hardness of the new-style wheels was increased by twice.

新型轮胎的耐磨硬度提高了两倍。

(七)…a n times (n-fold) + increase…

表示增加到 n 倍,可译为"增加了 n−1 倍"。

【例9】

There is a three times (three-fold) increase of computers in our ITS lab as compared with last year.

现在我们的ITS试验室的计算机台数比去年增加了两倍。

二、倍数减少的翻译法

(一)"减少了 n 倍"的表示法

可用"……系动词 + n times + 比较级 + than"表示,并译为"减少到 $\frac{1}{n+1}$"或"减少了 $\frac{n}{n+1}$"。

【例10】

Route A is 3 times shorter than route B.

路线A是路线B的1/4.(或译为:路线A比路线B短3/4。)

(二)"成 n 倍地减少"的表示法

1)表示减少意义的动词 + n times

可译为"减少到 1/n"或"减少了 $\frac{n-1}{n}$"。

【例11】

Switching time of new-type transistor is shortened 3 times.

新型晶体管的开关时间缩短了2/3。(或译为:新型晶体管的开关时间缩短到1/3。)

2)…a n times (n-fold) + reduction

【例12】

The length of A is a 3 times (three fold) reduction over that of B.

A的长度比B的长度缩短了2/3。(或译为:A的长度是B的长度的1/3。)

三、数量增减的其他表示法的翻译法

(一)…as + many(high,long,low…) + as + n

表示多(高、长、低……)达……之意。

【例 13】

The car's running speed on the way is as high as 140 km/h.

这辆小轿车在路上的运行速度高达 140 km/h。

(二)…(by)n + 名词 + 比较级 + than…

表示净增减,数字 n 照译。

【例 14】

Route A is (by) 10 meters longer than route B.

路线 A 比路线 B 长 10 m。

(三)表示增减意义的动词 + to + n

表示增加到 n 或减少到 n。

【例 15】

Computers have been increased to 20 in the lab.

实验室的计算机已经增加到了 20 台。

(四) too + 形容词

表示过于之意。

【例 16】

The line is too short by 2 centimeters. (The line is 2 centimeters too short.)

这条线的长度差 2 厘米。

(五)减少一半的翻译法

英语中,有些短语是表示减半之意的,如:cut / break / spit…in half (into halves) 把……切成(分成/分成)两半,decrease one - half 减去一半,one-half less 少一半 halve……将……减半,not half 少于一半地,be less than half 比一半还少,shorten…two times 缩短一半,等等。

【例 17】

The work completed is less than half.

所完成的工作还不到一半。

(六)分数的翻译法

分数由基数词 + 序数词构成,当分子大于一时,分母的序数词用复数。

例如:one third 三分之一;two thirds 三分之二;one (a) hundredth 百分之一;three twenty-fifths 二十五分之三;two and a half $2\frac{1}{2}$;three and a third $3\frac{1}{3}$;a few tenths of the given volume 给定体积的十分之几;等等。

【例 18】

We have finished two thirds of the project.

我们已经完成了该项目的 2/3。

论文写作技巧

在写学术论文时,应注意学术论文写作语法的特点和结构的组成。语法技巧将从学术论文通篇的语法特点进行介绍。学术论文的结构组成主要包括以下部分:

(1) Title and Author(s);
(2) Abstract;
(3) Keywords;
(4) Introduction;
(5) Methodology;
(6) Result;
(7) Discussions;
(8) Summary or Conclusion;
(9) Acknowledgements;
(10) Reference;
(11) Appendix。

技巧六:语法技巧

一、多用被动结构

专业英语的文章中,经常会发现一句话中有多个被动结构。这与其他文体不一样,专业英语很多时候不出现具体的主动者。

【例1】
If the transport of dangerous goods cannot be efficiently organized, it might result in personal or facilities injury or in destruction of equipment. Therefore, great care should be taken in transporting dangerous goods.

如果不能有效地组织危险货物的运输,就可能导致人身和设备的损伤,或者仪器的破坏,因此,危险货物的运输应特别当心。

上例由2个句子构成,共出现了3个谓语动词,而其中运用了被动结构(斜体部分)的就有2个。

二、多用动词非谓语结构

非谓语动词形式是指分词、动词不定式和动名词,交通工程专业文献中常用非谓语动词形式有如下两个主要原因:

(一)非谓语动词形式能使语言结构紧凑,行文简练

【例2】

Traffic engineer is concerned with the use of the highway by the road user and deals with matters relating to the regulation and control of vehicle and pedestrian traffic on new and existing facilities.

The scope of traffic engineering is wide, touching to some degree on each of the three E's —— Engineering, Enforcement, and Education.

上面两个例中,relating to 后面的部分作 matters 的定语,touching to 后面作状语。这两个分词短语,如果不用非谓语形式,只能用 which are related to…. 和 it is touched to …等从句形式,那样会使语句冗长,不符合交通专业文献的行文要求,即无法以最少的篇幅表达最多的重要信息。

(二)非谓语动词形式能体现和区分出句中信息的重要程度

【例3】

Selective-call telephone using open-wire pole lines were used for dispatching.

(铁路上)用明线电杆线路,靠选择呼叫电话来进行调度。

上例中谓语动词 were used 表达了主要信息,现在分词短语 using…提供细节,即非重要信息。这是定时动词和非谓语动词在表达信息功能上的主要分工和区别。

三、多用一般过去时

论文中不同的内容要考虑使用不同的时态,一般而言,交通专业文献主要反映与该领域有关的科学现象、规律、作业过程等,由于其客观性通常使用现在时态。而当论文叙述作者做了哪些研究工作,研究对象的情况,得出了什么结果,则主要用一般过去时。

【例4】

Bus Rapid Transit has been increasingly regarded as a cost-effective solution for improving mobility and alleviating congestion in urban transportation networks. Our research was aimed at providing a comprehensive guideline for planning and designing BRT that allows development of a BRT scenario in the traditional alternatives analysis. Specifically, this research developed a decision procedure to help engineers decide the role of BRT as an integral part of existing/future transportation systems. Design criteria was developed for BRT concepts, including possible street realignment, geometric considerations, right-of-way acquisition, signal preemption, dedicated/shared busways on major state arterials, as well as integration of BRT into existing and future managed lanes (HOT/HOV).

四、名词化特点显著

名词化特点主要是指在交通工程的文献中广泛使用能表示动作和状态的名词,或是起

名词作用的非限定动词。

【例5】

In the initial stages of road design it is usual for several alternative route proposals to be considered but only outline details of road center lines and estimates of speeds and flows are available.

在道路设计的初始阶段,通常有多种备选的路线方案需要考虑,但只需道路中线的概要数据和车速及流量的预测值。

【例6】

The testing of the air pollution should be considered in highway management.

在公路管理中,应该考虑进行空气污染测试。

以上两例表明,在交通工程专业文献中,名词一般从动词或形容词派生或转化而来,表示动作;名词一般以名词短语结构出行,典型结构为 n. + of + n.；而且名词还多出现连用的情况,即中心词之前有一个以上其他名词,它们皆以中心名词的前置修饰语,以简化句子结构,便于理解。

五、多用语体正式的词汇

英语中有很多意义灵活的动词短语,而交通工程专业英语文献中则多用与之对应的意义明确的单个词构成的动词。这类动词除了意义明确、精炼的特点外,还具有语体庄重、正式的特点。下面是一组对照,横线右边的词汇更适合于交通工程专业英语文献。

to use up——to exhaust　　　　to take up, to take in——to absorb
to push into——to insert　　　　to speed up——to accelerate
to put in——to addto　　　　　carry out——to perform
to use up——to consume　　　　to breathe in——to inhale
to think about——to consider　　to find out—— to discover
to take away——to remove　　　to get together——to concentrate
to drive forward——to propel　　to fill up——to occupy
to keep up——to maintain

同时,单个的英语词汇也有正式和非正式之分,交通工程专业英语文献属于正式文体,因此多用正式词汇。下面是一组对照,横线左边为非正式用语,右边为正式用语。

finish——complete　　　　　　oversee——supervise
underwater——submarine　　　hide——conceal
buy——purchase　　　　　　　enough——sufficient
similar——identical　　　　　　inner——interior
handbook——manual　　　　　help——assist
careful——cautious　　　　　　try——attempt
stop——cease　　　　　　　　get——obtain
deep——profound　　　　　　 leave——depart
before about——approximately　use——employ/utilize

技巧七：论文的题目与作者

一、题名（Title）

题名又称题目或标题。题名是以最恰当、最简明的词语反映论文中最重要的特定内容的逻辑组合。论文题目是一篇论文给出的涉及论文范围与水平的第一个重要信息，也是必须考虑到有助于选定关键词不达意和编制题录、索引等二次文献可以提供检索的特定实用信息。论文题目十分重要，必须用心斟酌选定。有人描述其重要性，称"论文题目是文章的一半"。论文题目要求准确得体、简短精练、外延和内涵恰如其分、醒目。

（一）准确得体

要求论文题目能准确表达论文内容，恰当反映所研究的范围和深度。常见毛病是：过于笼统，题不扣文。关键问题在于题目要紧扣论文内容，或论文内容与论文题目要互相匹配、紧扣，即题要扣文，文也要扣题。这是撰写论文的基本准则。一般不使用装饰型词组，例如 on the…，regarding…，investigation on…，the method of…，some thoughts on…，a research of…，避免使标题冗长。

【例1】

The Architecture of Intelligent Transportation Systems

上面例子中的题目太广，不具体，不准确，建议改成"The Architecture of Intelligent Transportation Systems — Vehicular Communication Options"。

【例2】

Safety and Productivity Improvement of Railroad Operations

根据内容建议改为：Safety and Productivity Improvement of Railroad Operations by Advanced Train Control System

避免使用问题标题，如 Is it…? Should be…? 等，不利于检索。如果必须要用疑问含义，可用不定词形式加问号。

【例3】

Onion Routers: A Dangerous Response to Traffic Analysis?

（二）简短精练

力求题目的字数要少，用词需要精选。至于多少字算是合乎要求，并无统一的硬性规定，但一般一篇论文题目不超出20个字。也不能由于一味追求字数少而影响题目对内容的恰当反映，在遇到两者确有矛盾时，宁可多用几个字也要力求表达明确。若简短题名不足以显示论文内容或反映出属于系列研究的性质，则可利用正、副标题的方法解决，以加副标题来补充说明特定的范围、方法及内容等信息。采用的缩写应是国际通用的标准缩写，避免使用不标准的缩写和符号。

（三）外延和内涵要恰如其分

外延和内涵属于形式逻辑中的概念。所谓外延，是指一个概念所反映的每一个对象；而所谓内涵，则是指对每一个概念对象特有属性的反映。命题时，若不考虑逻辑上有关外延和内涵的恰当运用，则有可能出现谬误，至少是不当。

(四) 醒目

论文题目虽然居于首先映入读者眼帘的醒目位置,但仍然存在题目是否醒目的问题,因为题目所用字句及其所表现的内容是否醒目,其产生的效果是相距甚远的。

以下一些题目不是好的题目:

"Some Problems in the Traffic Image Analysis"不醒目、不突出论文的关键技术和方法;
"Investigation on ITS technologies in Traffic Engineering"题目太泛太广,不适合作为期刊论文或会议论文的题目。

二、作者姓名和单位(Author(s) and affiliation(s))

论文的署名一是为了表明文责自负,二是记录劳动成果,三是便于读者与作者的联系及文献检索(作者索引)。大致分为二种情形,即:单个作者论文和多作者论文。后者按署名顺序列为第一作者、第二作者等。重要的是坚持实事求是的态度,对研究工作与论文撰写实际贡献最大的列为第一作者,贡献次之的,列为第二作者,以此类推。注明作者所在单位同样是为了便于读者与作者的联系。

英文的学术论文写作时要区分作者的姓和名,一般作者不要超过四个人,作者和作者信息的书写格式由所投期刊的具体要求而定。例如下面的图中为期刊 Transportation Research Part B 的作者和附属信息的写法。

PERGAMON   Transportation Research Part B 36 (2002) 19–35

TRANSPORTATION RESEARCH PART B

www.elsevier.com/locate/trb

Benefit distribution and equity in road network design

Qiang Meng, Hai Yang *

Department of Civil Engineering, The Hong Kong University of Science and Technology, Clear Water Bay, Kowloon, Hong Kong

Received 6 December 1999; received in revised form 7 June 2000; accepted 9 June 2000

Abstract

In the classical continuous network design problem, the optimal capacity enhancements are determined by minimizing the total system cost under a budget constraint, while taking into account the route choice behavior of network users. Generally the equilibrium origin–destination travel costs for some origin–destination (O–D) pairs may be increased after implementing these optimal capacity enhancements, leading to positive or negative results for network users. Therefore, the equity issue about the benefit gained from the network design problem is raised. In this paper, we examine the benefit distribution among the network

➡技巧八:摘要与关键词

一、摘要(Abstract)

论文一般应有摘要。它是对论文的内容不加注释和评论的简短陈述。其作用主要是为读者阅读、信息检索提供方便。摘要不宜太详尽,也不宜太简短,应将论文的研究体系、主要方法、重要发现、主要结论等,简明扼要地加以概括。

摘要主要描写下述内容:

(1)研究目的——准确描述该研究的目的,说明提出问题的缘由,表明研究的范围和重要性。

(2)研究方法——简要说明研究课题的基本设计,结论是如何得到的。

(3)结果——简要列出该研究的主要结果,有什么新发现,说明其价值和局限。叙述要具体、准确并给出结果的置信值。

(4)结论——简要地说明经验,论证取得的正确观点及理论价值或应用价值,是否还有与此有关的其他问题有待进一步研究,是否可推广应用等。

句子的组成结构可以按照五个部分进行组织:

$$\text{Abstract} = A1 + A2 + A3 + A4 + A5$$

A1:一个句子:文章主要涉及的知识领域和研究范围是什么?
A2:一个主题句:文章研究主题是什么?
A3:两到三个支持句:计算方法是什么?
A4:一个句子:得到的主要结论是什么?
A5:一个句子:文章的贡献是什么?
A2、A3、A4 常用的形式化的结构如下:

(1)主题句

The purpose of this paper is...

The primary goal of this research is...

The intention of this paper is to survey...

The overall objective of this study is...

The authors are now initiating some experimental investigation to establish...

The work presented in this paper focuses on several aspects of the following...

The emphasis of this study lies in...

(2)支持句

支持句一般紧随主题句之后,进一步具体化文章主题。

包括:研究方法、实验、程序、调查、计算、分析、结果及其其他重要信息,是摘要的主体。

The method used in this study is known as...

The technique is referred to as...

The procedure can be briefly described as...

The approach adopted is called...

The fundamental feature of this theory is as follows.

Recent experiments in this area suggested that...

Examples with actual experiment demonstrate...

(3)结论句

结论句通常分析结果,指出研究的重要性。

It's concluded that...
The results of the experiment indicated that...
The studies showed that...
The research suggested that...
The investigation carried out by... revealed that...
This work gives explanation of...

摘要的撰写要求：

(1)确保客观而充分地表述论文的内容,适当强调研究中创新、重要之处,但不要使用评价性语言;尽量包括论文中的主要论点和重要细节如重要的论证或数据等。不要照搬论文正文中的小标题(目录)或论文结论部分的文字。

(2)要求结构严谨、语义确切、表述简明、一般不分段落;表述要注意逻辑性,尽量使用指示性的词语来表达论文的不同部分,如使用"The methord is..."表示方法;使用"It is proposed that..."表示提出的结果等。

(3)排除在本学科领域方面已成为常识的或科普知识的内容;尽量避免引用文献,若无法回避使用引文,应在引文出现的位置将引文的书目信息标注在方括号内;不使用非本专业的读者尚难于清楚理解的缩略语、简称、代号,如确有需要(如避免多次重复较长的术语)使用非同行熟知的缩写,应在缩写符号第一次出现时给出其全称;不使用一次文献中列出的章节号、图、表号、公式号以及参考文献号。

(4)要求使用法定计量单位以及正确地书写规范字和标点符号;众所周知的国家、机构、专用术语尽可能用简称或缩写;为方便检索系统转录,应尽量避免使用图、表、化学结构式、数学表达式、角标和希腊文等特殊符号。

(5)摘要的长度:ISO 规定,大多数实验研究性文章,字数在 1000～5000 字的,其摘要长度限于 100～250 个英文单词。用词简化,例如"not only... but also"改为"and","from the results it can be concluded that"改为"the results show",写作中经常会出现"分析研究",不要翻译成"are analyzed and studied",这样翻译重复累赘,直接写成"are analyzed"就可以。

(6)摘要的时态:摘要所采用的时态因情况而定,应力求表达自然、妥当。写作中可大致遵循以下原则:①介绍背景资料时,如果句子的内容是不受时间影响的普遍事实,应使用现在时;如果句子的内容为对某种研究趋势的概述,则使用现在完成时。②在叙述研究目的或主要研究活动时,如果采用"论文的研究导向",多使用过去时(如:This paper presented...)。

(7)摘要的人称和语态:作为一种可阅读和检索的独立使用的文体,摘要一般只用第三人称而不用其他人称来写。有的摘要出现了"我们"、"作者"作为陈述的主语,这会减弱摘要表述的客观性,有时也会出现逻辑不通。

二、关键词(Keywords)

关键词是为了适应计算机检索的需要而提出来的,位置在摘要之后。早在 1963 年,美国 Chemical Abstracts 从第 58 卷起,就开始采用电子计算机编制关键词索引,提供快速检索文献资料主题的途径。在科学技术信息迅猛发展的今天,全世界每天有几十万篇科技论文发表,学术界早已约定利用主题概念词去检索最新发表的论文。作者发表的论文不标注关键词或叙词,文献数据库就不会收录此类文章,读者就检索不到。关键词选得是否恰当,关系到该文被检索和该成果的利用率。

　　国际标准和我国标准均要求论文摘要后标引 3～8 个关键词。关键词既可以作为文献检索或分类的标识,它本身又是论文主题的浓缩。读者从中可以判断论文的主题、研究方向、方法等。关键词包括主题词和自由词两类:主题词是专门为文献的标引或检索而从自然语言的主要词汇中挑选出来的,并加以规范化了的词或词组;自由词则是未规范的即还未收入主题词表中的词或词组。关键词以名词或名词短语居多,如果使用缩略词,则应为公认和普遍使用的缩略语,如 IP、CAD、CPU,否则应写出全称,其后用括号标出其缩略语形式。

　　关键词或主题词的一般选择方法是由作者在完成论文写作后,纵观全文,选出能表示论文主要内容的信息或词汇,这些注处或词汇,可以从论文标题中去找和选,也可以从论文内容中去找和选。例如上例,关键词选用了 6 个,其中前三个就是从论文标题中选出的,而后三个却是从论文内容中选取出来的。后三个关键词的选取,补充了论文标题所未能表示出的主要内容信息,也提高了所涉及的概念深度。需要选出,与从标题中选出的关键词一道组成该论文的关键词组。

(一)关键词分类

关键词包括叙词和自由词。

(1)叙词——指收入《汉语主题词表》、《MeSH》等词表中可用于标引文献主题概念的经过规范化的词或词组。

(2)自由词——反映该论文主题中新技术、新学科尚未被主题词表收录的新产生的名词术语或在叙词表中找不到的词。

(二)关键词标引

为适应计算机自动检索的需要,GB/T 3179—92 规定,现代科技期刊都应在学术论文的摘要后面给出 3～8 个关键词(或叙词)。关键词的标引应按《文献叙词标引规则》(GB/T 3860——1995)的原则和方法,参照各种词表和工具书选取;未被词表收录的新学科、新技术中的重要术语以及文章题名的人名、地名也可作为关键词标出。

　　所谓标引,系指对文献和某些具有检索意义的特征如:研究对象,处理方法和实验设备等进行主题分析,并利用主题词表给出主题检索标识的过程。对文献进行主题分析,是为了从内容复杂的文献中通过分析找出构成文献主题的基本要素,以便准确地标引所需的叙词。标引是检索的前提,没有正确的标引,也就不可能有正确的检索。科技论文应按照叙词的标引方法标引关键词,并尽可能将自由词规范为叙词。

(三)标引关键词应遵循的基本原则

1. 专指性原则

　　一个词只能表达一个主题概念为专指性。只要在叙词表中找到相应的专指性叙词,就不允许用词表中的上位词(S 项)或下位词(F 项);若找不到与主题概念直接对应的叙词,而上位词确实与主题概念相符,即可选用。例如:"飞机防火"在叙词表中可以找到相应的专指词"专机防火",那么就必须优先选用。不得用其上位词"防火"标引,也不得用"飞机"与"防火"这两个主题词组配标引。

2. 自由词标引

下列几种情况关键词允许采用自由词标引。

(1) 主题词表中明显漏选的主题概念词。

(2) 表达新学科、新理论、新技术、新材料等新出现的概念。

(3) 词表中未收录的地区、人物、产品等名称及重要数据名称。

(4) 某些概念采用组配,其结果出现多义时,被标引概念也可用自由词标引。自由词尽可能选自其他词或较权威的参考书和工具书,选用的自由词必须达到词形简练、概念明确、实用性强。

(四) 关键词的标引步骤

首先对文献进行主题分析,弄清该文的主题概念和中心内容;尽可能从题名、摘要、层次标题和正文的重要段落中抽出与主题概念一致的词和词组;对所选出的词进行排序,对照叙词表找出哪些词可以直接作为叙词标引,哪些词可以通过规范化变为叙词,哪些叙词可以组配成专指主题概念的词组;还有相当数量无法规范为叙词的词,只要是表达主题概念所必需的,都可作为自由词标引并列入关键词。尽量使用名词而不是动词,如用 fabrication 而不是 fabricate。

在关键词标引中,应很好地利用《汉语主题词表》和其他《叙词表》,标引过程应该查表;切忌主题概念分析和词的组配有误;要控制自由词标引的数量。有英文摘要的论文,应在英文摘要的下方著录与中文关键词相对应的英文关键词。

关键词书写时一般第一个单词首字母大写,词间用",",或者";"隔开。例如下图:

PERGAMON Transportation Research Part B 36 (2002) 19–35

TRANSPORTATION
RESEARCH
PART B

www.elsevier.com/locate/trb

Benefit distribution and equity in road network design

Qiang Meng, Hai Yang *

*Department of Civil Engineering, The Hong Kong University of Science and Technology,
Clear Water Bay, Kowloon, Hong Kong*

Received 6 December 1999; received in revised form 7 June 2000; accepted 9 June 2000

Abstract

In the classical continuous network design problem, the optimal capacity enhancements are determined by minimizing the total system cost under a budget constraint, while taking into account the route choice behavior of network users. Generally the equilibrium origin–destination travel costs for some origin–destination (O–D) pairs may be increased after implementing these optimal capacity enhancements, leading to positive or negative results for network users. Therefore, the equity issue about the benefit gained from the network design problem is raised. In this paper, we examine the benefit distribution among the network users and the resulting equity associated with the continuous network design problem in terms of the change of equilibrium O–D travel costs. Bilevel programming models that incorporate the equity constraint are proposed for the continuous network design problem. A penalty function approach by embodying a simulated annealing method is used to test the models for a network example. © 2001 Elsevier Science Ltd. All rights reserved.

Keywords: Equity; Network design; Optimization; User equilibrium; Bilevel programming

⬢技巧九：论文主体

一、引言（Introduction）

引言又称前言，属于整篇论文的引论部分，位于正文的起始部分，主要叙述自己写作的目的或研究的宗旨，使读者了解和评估研究成果。主要内容包括：介绍相关研究的历史、现状、进展，说明自己对已有成果的看法，以往工作的不足之处，以及自己所做研究的创新性或重要价值；说明研究中要解决的问题、所采取的方法，必要时须说明采用某种方法的理由；介绍论文的主要结果和结构安排。

引言的文字不可冗长，内容选择不必过于分散、琐碎，措辞要精练，要吸引读者读下去。引言的篇幅大小，并无硬性的统一规定，需视整篇论文篇幅的大小及论文内容的需要来确定，长的可达 700~800 字或 1000 字左右，短的可不到 100 字。

二、正文（Main body）

正文是一篇论文的本论，属于论文的主体，它占据论文的最大篇幅。论文所体现的创造性成果或新的研究结果，都将在这一部分得到充分的反映。因此，要求这一部分内容充实，论据充分、可靠，论证有力，主题明确。为了满足这一系列要求，同时也为了做到层次分明、脉络清晰，常常将正文部分分成几个大的段落。这些段落即所谓逻辑段，一个逻辑段可包含几个自然段。每一逻辑段落可冠以适当标题（分标题或小标题）。段落和划分，应视论文性质与内容而定。

（一）正文书写中需要注意以下几点

（1）准确、清楚且简洁地指出所探讨问题的本质和范围，对研究背景的阐述做到繁简适度。

（2）在背景介绍和问题的提出中，应引用"最相关"的文献以指引读者。要优先选择引用的文献包括相关研究中的经典、重要和最具说服力的文献，力戒刻意回避引用最重要的相关文献（甚至是对作者研究具某种"启示"性意义的文献），或者不恰当地大量引用作者本人的文献。

（3）采取适当的方式强调作者在本次研究中最重要的发现或贡献，让读者顺着逻辑的演进阅读论文。

（4）解释或定义专门术语或缩写词，以帮助编辑、审稿人和读者阅读稿件。

（5）尽量不要使用主观的语气，叙述前人工作的欠缺以强调自己研究的创新时，应慎重且留有余地。可采用类似如下的表达：To the author's knowledge...；There is little information available in literature about…；Until recently, there is some lack of knowledge about... 等等。

（6）时态运用：

①叙述有关现象或普遍事实时，句子的主要动词多使用现在时，如："little is known about X"或"little literature is available on X"。

②描述特定研究领域中最近的某种趋势，或者强调表示某些"最近"发生的事件对现在

的影响时,常采用现在完成时,如:"few studies have been done on X"或"little attention has been devoted to X"。

③在阐述作者本人研究目的的句子中应有类似 This paper,The experiment reported here 等词,以表示所涉及的内容是作者的工作,而不是指其他学者过去的研究。例如:"In summary, previous methods are all extremely inefficient. Hence a new approach is developed to process the data more efficiently."就容易使读者产生误解,其中的第二句应修改为:"In this paper, a new approach will be developed to process the data more efficiently."或者,"This paper will present (presents) a new approach that process the data more efficiently."。

(二)研究过程和方法的说明

在论文中,这一部分用于说明研究的对象、条件、使用的材料、步骤或计算的过程、公式的推导、模型的建立等。对过程的描述要完整具体,符合其逻辑步骤,以便读者重复实验。

具体要求如下:

(1)对材料的描述应清楚、准确。材料描述中应该清楚地指出研究对象(样品或产品、动物、植物、病人)的数量、来源和准备方法。对于实验材料的名称,应采用国际同行所熟悉的通用名,尽量避免使用只有作者所在国家的人所熟悉专门名称。

(2)对方法的描述要详略得当、重点突出。应遵循的原则是给出足够的细节信息以便让同行能够重复实验,避免混入有关结果或发现方面的内容。如果方法新颖且不曾发表过,应提供所有必需的细节;如果所采用的方法已经公开报道过,引用相关的文献即可(如果报道该方法期刊的影响力很有限,可稍加详细地描述)。

(3)力求语法正确、描述准确。由于材料和方法部分通常需要描述很多的内容,因此通常需要采用很简洁的语言,故使用精确的英语描述材料和方法是十分重要的。需要注意的方面通常有:

①不要遗漏动作的执行者,如:"To determine its respiratory quotient, the organism was..."，显然,the organism 不能来 determine;又如:"Having completed the study, the bacteria were of no further interest."，显然,the bacteria 不会来 completed the study。

②在简洁表达的同时要注意内容方面的逻辑性。

③如果有多种可供选择的方法能采用,在引用文献时提及一下具体的方法,如:"cells were broken by as previously described[9]" 不够清楚,应改为:"cells were broken by ultrasonic treatment as previously described[9]"。

(4)时态与语态的运用:

①若描述的内容为不受时间影响的事实,采用一般现在时,如:A twin-lens reflex camera is actually a combination of two separate camera boxes。

②若描述的内容为特定、过去的行为或事件,则采用过去式,如:The work was carried out on the Imperial College gas atomizer, which has been described in detail elsewhere[4,5]。

③方法章节的焦点在于描述实验中所进行的每个步骤以及所采用的材料,由于所涉及的行为与材料是讨论的焦点,而且读者已知道进行这些行为和采用这些材料的人就是作者自己,因而一般都习惯采用被动语态。例如:

优:The samples were immersed in an ultrasonic bath for 3 minutes in acetone followed by 10 minutes in distilled water.

劣：We immersed the samples in an ultrasonic bath for 3 minutes in acetone followed by 10 minutes in distilled water.

④如果涉及表达作者的观点或看法，则应采用主动语态。例如：

优：For the second trial, the apparatus was covered by a sheet of plastic. We believed this modification would reduce the amount of scattering.

优：For the second trial, the apparatus was covered by a sheet of plastic to reduce the amount of scattering.

劣：For the second trial, the apparatus was covered by a sheet of plastic. It was believed that this modification would reduce the amount of scattering.

(三)研究的结果

研究结果可自成体系，读者不必参考论文其他部分，也能了解作者的研究成果。对结果的叙述也要按照其逻辑顺序进行，使其既符合实验过程的逻辑顺序，又符合实验结果的推导过程。本部分还可以包括对实验结果的分类整理和对比分析等。

写作要求如下：

(1)对实验或观察结果的表达要高度概括和提炼，不能简单地将实验记录数据或观察事实堆积到论文中，尤其是要突出有科学意义和具代表性的数据，而不是没完没了地重复一般性数据。

(2)对实验结果的叙述要客观真实，即使得到的结果与实验不符，也不可略而不述，而且还应在讨论中加以说明和解释。

(3)数据表达可采用文字与图表相结合的形式。如果只有一个或很少的测定结果，在正文中用文字描述即可；如果数据较多，可采用图表形式来完整、详细地表述，文字部分则用来指出图表中资料的重要特性或趋势。切忌在文字中简单地重复图表中的数据，而忽略叙述其趋势、意义以及相关推论。

(4)适当解释原始数据，以帮助读者理解。尽管对于研究结果的详细讨论主要出现在"讨论"章节，但"结果"中应该提及必要的解释，以便让读者能清楚地了解作者此次研究结果的意义或重要性。

(5)文字表达应准确、简洁、清楚。避免使用冗长的词汇或句子来介绍或解释图表。为简洁、清楚起见，不要把图表的序号作为段落的主题句，应在句子中指出图表所揭示的结论，并把图表的序号放入括号中。例如，"Figure 1 shows the relationship between A and B"不如"A was significantly higher than B at all time points hecked (Figure 1)"，又如，"It is clearly shown in Table 1 that nocillin inhibited the growth of N. gonorrhoeae."不如"Nocillin inhibited the growth of N. gonorrhoeae (Table 1)."。

(6)时态的运用：

①指出结果在哪些图表中列出，常用一般现在时，如：Figure 2 shows the variation in the temperature of the samples over time.

②叙述或总结研究结果的内容为关于过去的事实，所以通常采用过去时，如：After flights of less than two hours, 11% of the army pilots and 33% of the civilian pilots reported back pain.

③对研究结果进行说明或由其得出一般性推论时,多用现在时,如:The higher incidence of back pain in civilian pilots may be due to their greater accumulated flying time.

④不同结果之间或实验数据与理论模型之间进行比较时,多采用一般现在时(这种比较关系多为不受时间影响的逻辑上的事实),如:These results agree well with the findings of Smith, et al.

(四)讨论部分

"讨论"的重点在于对研究结果的解释和推断,并说明作者的结果是否支持或反对某种观点、是否提出了新的问题或观点等。因此撰写讨论时要避免含蓄,尽量做到直接、明确,以便审稿人和读者了解论文为什么值得引起重视。讨论的内容主要有:

①回顾研究的主要目的或假设,并探讨所得到的结果是否符合原来的期望?如果没有,为什么?

②概述最重要的结果,并指出其是否能支持先前的假设以及是否与其他学者的结果相互一致;如果不是,为什么?

③对结果提出说明、解释或猜测;根据这些结果,能得出何种结论或推论?

④指出研究的限制以及这些限制对研究结果的影响,并建议进一步的研究题目或方向;

⑤指出结果的理论意义(支持或反驳相关领域中现有的理论、对现有理论的修正)和实际应用。

具体的写作要求如下:

(1)对结果的解释要重点突出,简洁、清楚。为有效地回答研究问题,可适当简要地回顾研究目的并概括主要结果,但不能简单地罗列结果,因为这种结果的概括是为讨论服务的。

(2)推论要符合逻辑,避免实验数据不足以支持的观点和结论。根据结果进行推理时要适度,论证时一定要注意结论和推论的逻辑性。在探讨实验结果或观察事实的相互关系和科学意义时,无需得出试图去解释一切的巨大结论。如果把数据外推到一个更大的、不恰当的结论,不仅无益于提高作者的科学贡献,甚至现有数据所支持的结论也受到怀疑。

(3)观点或结论的表述要清楚、明确。尽可能清楚地指出作者的观点或结论,并解释其支持还是反对早先的工作。结束讨论时,避免使用诸如"Future studies are needed."之类苍白无力的句子。

(4)对结果科学意义和实际应用效果的表达要实事求是,适当留有余地。避免使用"For the first time"等类似的优先权声明。在讨论中应选择适当的词汇来区分推测与事实。例如,可选用"prove","demonstrate"等表示作者坚信观点的真实性;选用"show","indicate","found"等表示作者对问题的答案有某些不确定性;选用"imply","suggest"等表示推测;或者选用情态动词"can","will","should","probably","may","could","possibly"等来表示论点的确定性程度。

(5)时态的运用:

①回顾研究目的时,通常使用过去时。如:In this study, the effects of two different learning methods were investigated.

②如果作者认为所概述结果的有效性只是针对本次特定的研究,需用过去时;相反,如果具有普遍的意义,则用现在时。如:In the first series of trials, the experimental values were all lower than the theoretical predictions. The experimental and theoretical values for the yields agree well.

③阐述由结果得出的推论时,通常使用现在时。使用现在时的理由是作者得出的是具普遍有效的结论或推论(而不只是在讨论自己的研究结果),并且结果与结论或推论之间的逻辑关系为不受时间影响的事实。如:The data reported here suggest (These findings support the hypothesis, our data provide evidence) that the reaction rate may be determined by the amount of oxygen available.

(五) 总结

作者在文章的最后要单独用一章或一节对全文进行总结,其主要内容是对研究的主要发现和成果进行概括总结,让读者对全文的重点有一个深刻的印象。有的文章也在本部分提出当前研究的不足之处,对研究的前景和后续工作进行展望。应注意的是,撰写结论时不应涉及前文不曾指出的新事实,也不能在结论中重复论文中其他章节中的句子,或者叙述其他不重要或与自己研究没有密切联系的内容,以故意把结论拉长。

(六) 致谢

论文作者可以在论文末尾对他人给予自己的指导和帮助表示感谢即致谢,一般置于结论之后,参考文献之前。其基本形式如下:

致谢者,被致谢者,致谢的原因

例如:L. Wu is very grateful to the National Science Foundation of China (NNSFC) for the support.

也可以是作者具体指出某人做了什么工作使研究工作得以完成,从而表示谢意。

如果作者既要感谢某机构、团体、企业或个人的经济资助,又要感谢他人的技术、设备的支持,则应按惯例先对经济资助表示感谢,再对技术、设备支持表示感谢。

致谢的文字表达要朴素、简洁,以显示其严肃和诚意。

技巧十:英文参考文献的写法

参考文献主要是便于进行文献检索,体现了对于他人劳动成果的尊重。标注的参考文献必须是真实的出版物。关于参考文献的内容和格式,建议作者在把握参考文献注录基本原则的前提下,参阅所投刊物的"投稿须知"中对参考文献的要求,或同一刊物的其他论文参考文献的注录格式,使自己论文的文献列举和标注方法与所刊物相一致。常用的书写规范可以参考"The Numeric System"和"The Harvard System"。这里只对基本规则作简单介绍。

ISO 5966—1982 中规定参考文献应包含以下三项内容:作者/题目/有关出版事项。其中出版事项包括:书刊名称、出版地点、出版单位、出版年份以及卷、期、页等。

一、参考文献的编排顺序

参考文献的编排顺序有如下两种:

(1) 按作者姓氏字母顺序排列(alphabetical list of references);

(2) 按序号编排(numbered list of references),即对各参考文献按引用的顺序编排序号,正文中引用时只要写明序号即可,无需列出作者姓名和出版年代。

目前常用的正文和参考文献的标注格式有三种:

(1)MLA参考文献格式:MLA参考文献格式由美国现代语言协会(Modern Language Association)制定,适合人文科学类论文,其基本格式为:在正文标注参考文献作者的姓和页码,文末间列参考文献项,以Works Cited为标题。

(2)APA参考文献格式:APA参考文献格式由美国心理学会(American Psychological Association)制定,多适用于社会科学和自然科学类论文,其基本格式为:正文引用部分注明参考文献作者姓氏和出版时间,文末单列参考文献项,以References为标题。

(3)Chicago参考文献格式:该格式由芝加哥大学出版社(University of Chicago Press)制定,可用于人文科学类和自然科学类论文,其基本格式为:正文中按引用先后顺序连续编排序号,在该页底以脚注(Footnotes)或在文末以尾注(Endnotes)形式注明出处,或在文末单列参考文献项,以Bibliography为标题。

二、参考文献的分类

在交通工程专业的论文中引用和标注的参考文献主要有以下五类:专著(M)、科技期刊(J)、会议论文集(C)、学位论文(D)、网络文献(W)。

(一)专著类

专著类的参考文献中需要写的信息包括:

Author(s)、Title、Edition(if applicable)、Place of publication、Publisher、Date。

【例1】

Claude, J. Isaiah Berlin's Liberalism. Oxford, Clarendon Press, 1994.

注:姓在前时,姓和名间要加",",名字若采用缩写要有缩写符号。

当有作者同时还有编者时,可以写成:

【例2】

Shakespeare, W. The Tragedy of Macbeth. Ed. Louis B. Wright. New York:Washington Square, 1959.

(二)期刊论文类

书写期刊论文作为参考文献时,需要写的信息包括:

Author(s)、Title of the article、Title of the periodical、or its accepted abbreviation、Date、Volume、Part number of the issue in which it appears、Page numbers。

【例3】

Yu, N. A., et al. Gas Detonation and its Application in Engineering and Technologies. Journal of Combustion, Explosion, and Shock Waves, 2003, Vol. 39(4), 382-410.

注:当作者超过3个人时,可以只写第一个作者,其余作者用"et al."代表。

(三)会议论文类

书写会议论文作为参考文献时和期刊论文类似,但需要说明会议的信息,主要信息包括:

Author(s)、Title of the article、Title of the proceeding、Place of the conference (if can find)、

Date、Volume、Part number of the issue in which it appears、Page numbers。

【例4】

Pietrzyk, M. C. & Perez, A. R. Solving Transportation Problems With Artificial Neural Networks. Proceedings of the 3rd World Congress on ITS. Orlando, Florida, 1996, Vol. 3(3), 34-37.

（四）学位论文类

主要信息包括：

Author、Title of the Dissertation、University、Date。

【例5】

Li, H. Light Rail Transit in China. Southwest Jiaotong University, 1999.

（五）网络文献类

现在的论文中经常会引用网络中的信息和资料,值得注意的是,引用的网络上的信息和资料必须为官方的资料或者经证实为真实可信的信息和资料。建议引用后缀为 org 或百科类的资料。标注网页信息为参考文献时,需要写明：

Author or source、Title、Website address、Cited date。

【例6】

Institute for Transportation and Development Policy. Bus Rapid Transit Planning Guide, 2008, http://www.itdp.org/index.php/microsite/brt_planning_guide/. [accessed June 12, 2008].

●技巧十一：论文撰写规范

　　语言和内容是评判一篇英语论文质量高低的重要依据,但写作格式规范与否也是一个不可忽略的衡量标准。因此,规范英语论文的格式,使其与国际学术惯例接轨,对从事英语教学、英语论文写作,促进国际学术交流都具有重要意义。由于英语论文写作规范随学科不同而各有所异,本文拟就人文类学科英语论文的主要组成部分,概述美国教育界、学术界通行的人文类英语论文写作规范,以供读者参考、仿效。

一、英语论文的标题

　　一篇较长的英语论文(如英语毕业论文)一般都需要标题页,其书写格式如下:第一行标题与打印纸顶端的距离约为打印纸全长的三分之一,与下行(通常为 by,居中)的距离则为 5cm,第三、第四行分别为作者姓名及日期(均居中)。如果该篇英语论文是学生针对某门课程而写,则在作者姓名与日期之间还需分别打上教师学衔及其姓名(如:Dr./Prof. C. Prager)及本门课程的编号或名称(如:English 734 或 British Novel)。打印时,如无特殊要求,每一行均需 double space,即隔行打印,行距约为 0.6cm(论文其他部分行距同此)。

　　就学生而言,如果英语论文篇幅较短,也可不做标题页(及提纲页),而将标题页的内容打在正文第一页的左上方。第一行为作者姓名,与打印纸顶端距离约为 2.5cm,以下各行依次为教师学衔和姓、课程编号(或名称)及日期;各行左边上下对齐,并留出 2.5cm 左右的页边空白(下同)。接下来便是论文标题及正文(日期与标题之间及标题与正文第一行之间只需隔行打印,不必留出更多空白)。

二、英语论文提纲

英语论文提纲页包括论题句及提纲本身,其规范格式如下:先在第一行(与打印纸顶端的距离仍为2.5cm左右)的始端写上Thesis一词及冒号,空一格后再写论题句,回行时左边须与论题句的第一个字母上下对齐。主要纲目以大写罗马数字标出,次要纲目则依次用大写英文字母、阿拉伯数字和小写英文字母标出。各数字或字母后均为一句点,空出一格后再写该项内容的第一个字母;处于同一等级的纲目,其上下行左边必须对齐。需要注意的是,同等重要的纲目必须是两个以上,即:有Ⅰ应有Ⅱ,有A应有B,以此类推。如果英文论文提纲较长,需两页纸,则第二页须在右上角用小写罗马数字标出页码,即ii(第一页无需标页码)。

三、英语论文正文

有标题页和提纲页的英语论文,其正文第一页的规范格式为:论文标题居中,其位置距打印纸顶端约5cm,距正文第一行约1.5cm。段首字母需缩进五格,即从第六格写起。正文第一页不必标页码(但应计算其页数),自第二页起,必须在每页的右上角(即空出第一行,在其后部)写上论文作者的姓,空一格后再用阿拉伯数字标出页码;阿拉伯数字(或其最后一位)应为该行的最后一个空格。在书写正文时尚需注意标点符号的书写格式,即:句末号(句号、问号及感叹号)后应空两格,其他标点符号后则空一格。

四、英语论文的文中引述

正确引用作品原文或专家、学者的论述是写好英语论文的重要环节;既要注意引述与论文的有机统一,即其逻辑性,又要注意引述格式(即英语论文参考文献)的规范性。引述别人的观点,可以直接引用,也可以间接引用。无论采用何种方式,论文作者必须注明所引文字的作者和出处。目前美国学术界通行的做法是在引文后以圆括弧形式注明引文作者及出处。现针对文中引述的不同情况,将部分规范格式分述如下。

(1)若引文不足三行,则可将引文有机地融合在论文中。

【例1】

The divorce of Arnold's personal desire from his inheritance results in "the familiar picture of Victorian man alone in an alien universe" (Roper9).

这里,圆括弧中的Roper为引文作者的姓(不必注出全名);阿拉伯数字为引文出处的页码(不要写成p.9);作者姓与页码之间需空一格,但不需任何标点符号;句号应置于第二个圆括弧后。

(2)被引述的文字如果超过三行,则应将引文与论文文字分开,如下例所示:

【例2】

Whitman has proved himself an eminent democratic representative and precursor, and his "Democratic Vistas" is an admirable and characteristic diatribe. And if one is sorry that in it

Whitman is unable to conceive the extreme crises of society, one is certain that no society would be tolerable whoses citizens could not find refreshment in its buoyant democratic idealism. (Chase 165)

  这里的格式有两点要加以注意：
①引文各行距英语论文的左边第一个字母十个空格，即应从第十一格写起；
②是引文不需加引号，末尾的句号应标在最后一个词后。
（3）如需在引文中插注，对某些词语加以解释，则要使用方括号（不可用圆括号）。

【例3】

Dr. Beaman points out that "he [Charles Darwin] has been an important factor in the debate between evolutionary theory and biblical creationism" (9).

  值得注意的是，本例中引文作者的姓已出现在引导句中，故圆括号中只需注明引文出处的页码即可。
（4）如果拟引用的文字中有与论文无关的词语需要删除，则需用省略号。如果省略号出现在引文中则用三个点，如出现在引文末，则用四个点，最后一点表示句号，置于第二个圆括号后（一般说来，应避免在引文开头使用省略号）；点与字母之间，或点与点之间都需空一格。

【例4】

Mary Shelley hated tyranny and "looked upon the poor as pathetic victims of the social system and upon the rich and highborn... with undisguised scorn and contempt... (Nitchie 43).

（5）若引文出自一部多卷书，除注明作者姓和页码外，还需注明卷号。

【例5】

Professor Chen Jia's A History of English Literature aimed to give Chinese readers "a historical survey of English literature from its earliest beginnings down to the 20th century" (Chen, 1: i).

  圆括号里的1为卷号，小写罗马数字i为页码，说明引文出自第1卷序言（引言、序言、导言等多使用小写的罗马数字标明页码）。此外，书名 A History of English Literature 加了下划线；规范的格式是：书名，包括以成书形式出版的作品名（如《失乐园》）均需加下划线，或用斜体字；其他作品，如诗歌、散文、短篇小说等的标题则以双引号标出，如"To Autumn"及前面出现的"Democratic Vistas"等。
（6）如果英语论文中引用了同一作者的两篇或两篇以上的作品，除注明引文作者及页码外，还要注明作品名。

【例6】

Farrington points out that Aristotle's father Nicomachus, a physician, probably trained his son in medicine (Aristotle 15).

  这两个例子分别引用了 Farrington 的两部著作，故在各自的圆括号中分别注出所引用的书名，以免混淆。两部作品名均为缩写形式（如书名太长，在圆括号中加以注明时均需使用缩写形式），其全名分别为 Founder of Scientific Philosophy 及 The Philosophy of Francis Baconand Aristotle。
  以下为一个会议论文的格式要求范本：

Author Guidelines for 8.5 x 11-inch Proceedings Manuscripts

Author(s) Name(s)
Author Affiliation(s)
E-mail

Abstract

The abstract is to be in fully-justified italicized text, at the top of the left-hand column as it is here, below the author information. Use the word "Abstract" as the title, in 12-point Times, boldface type, centered relative to the column, initially capitalized. The abstract is to be in 10-point, single-spaced type, and up to 150 words in length. Leave two blank lines after the abstract, then begin the main text.

1. Introduction

All manuscripts must be in English. These guidelines include complete descriptions of the fonts, spacing, and related information for producing your proceedings manuscripts. Please follow them and if you have any questions, direct them to the production editor in charge of your proceedings at the IEEE Computer Society Press: Phone (714) 821-8380 or Fax (714) 761-1784.

2. Formatting your paper

All printed material, including text, illustrations, and charts, must be kept within a print area of 6-1/2 inches (16.51 cm) wide by 8-7/8 inches (22.51 cm) high. Do not write or print anything outside the print area. All *text* must be in a two-column format. Columns are to be 3-1/16 inches (7.85 cm) wide, with a 3/8 inch (0.81 cm) space between them. Text must be fully justified.

A format sheet with the margins and placement guides is available as both Word and PDF files as <format.doc> and <format.pdf>. It contains lines and boxes showing the margins and print areas. If you hold it and your printed page up to the light, you can easily check your margins to see if your print area fits within the space allowed.

3. Main title

The main title (on the first page) should begin 1-3/8 inches (3.49 cm) from the top edge of the page, centered, and in Times 14-point, boldface type. Capitalize the first letter of nouns, pronouns, verbs, adjectives, and adverbs; do not capitalize articles, coordinate conjunctions, or prepositions (unless the title begins with such a word). Leave two 12-point blank lines after the title.

4. Author name(s) and affiliation(s)

Author names and affiliations are to be centered beneath the title and printed in Times 12-point, non-boldface type. Multiple authors may be shown in a two- or three-column format, with their affiliations italicized and centered below their respective names. Include e-mail addresses if possible. Author information should be followed by two 12-point blank lines.

5. Second and following pages

The second and following pages should begin 1.0 inch (2.54 cm) from the top edge. On all pages, the bottom margin should be 1-1/8 inches (2.86 cm) from the bottom edge of the page for 8.5 x 11-inch paper; for A4 paper, approximately 1-5/8 inches (4.13 cm) from the bottom edge of the page.

6. Type-style and fonts

Wherever Times is specified, Times Roman or Times New Roman may be used. If neither is available on your word processor, please use the font closest in appearance to Times. Avoid using bit-mapped fonts if possible. True-Type 1 fonts are preferred.

7. Main text

Type your main text in 10-point Times, single-spaced. Do **not** use double-spacing. All paragraphs should be indented 1/4 inch (approximately 0.5 cm). Be sure your text is fully justified—that is, flush left and flush right. Please do not place any additional blank lines between paragraphs.

Figure and table captions should be 10-point boldface Helvetica (or a similar sans-serif font). Callouts should be 9-point non-boldface Helvetica. Initially capitalize only the first word of each figure caption and table title. Figures and tables must be numbered separately. For example: "Figure 1. Database contexts", "Table 1. Input data". Figure captions are to be centered *below* the figures. Table titles are to be centered *above* the tables.

8. First-order headings

For example, "1. Introduction", should be Times 12-point boldface, initially capitalized, flush left, with one blank line before, and one blank line after. Use a period (".") after the heading number, not a colon.

8.1. Second-order headings

As in this heading, they should be Times 11-point boldface, initially capitalized, flush left, with one blank line before, and one after.

8.1.1. Third-order headings. Third-order headings, as in this paragraph, are discouraged. However, if you must use them, use 10-point Times, boldface, initially capitalized, flush left, preceded by one blank line, followed by a period and your text on the same line.

9. Footnotes

Use footnotes sparingly (or not at all) and place them at the bottom of the column on the page on which they are referenced. Use Times 8-point type, single-spaced. To help your readers, avoid using footnotes altogether and include necessary peripheral observations in the text (within parentheses, if you prefer, as in this sentence).

10. References

List and number all bibliographical references in 9-point Times, single-spaced, at the end of your paper. When referenced in the text, enclose the citation number in square brackets, for example [1]. Where appropriate, include the name(s) of editors of referenced books.

[1] A.B. Smith, C.D. Jones, and E.F. Roberts, "Article Title", *Journal*, Publisher, Location, Date, pp. 1-10.

[2] Jones, C.D., A.B. Smith, and E.F. Roberts, *Book Title*, Publisher, Location, Date.

11. Copyright forms and reprint orders

You must include your fully-completed, signed IEEE copyright release form when you submit your paper. We **must** have this form before your paper can be published in the proceedings. The copyright form is available as a Word file, <copyright.doc>, as a PDF version, <copyright.pdf>, and as a text file in <authguid.txt>.

Reprints may be ordered using the form provided as <reprint.doc> or <reprint.pdf>.

Key to Exercises

● Part I

Chapter 1

I. True or false.

1. T   2. F   3. T   4. T   5. F

II. Choose the best word or phrase to complete each statement.

1. C   2. B   3. A   4. B   5. D

III. Translate the following sentences into Chinese.

1. 同样,机动性给出行者提供多种出行目的的选择,包括休闲旅游、就医、上学,甚至包括上班的通勤。

2. 然而车辆的位移不是目的,目的在于运送占据车辆的人和货物。

3. 研究集中于数据收集和分析,这些可以用于描述交通的特性,包括(但不局限于)交通量和交通需求、车速和出行时间、延误、事故、起讫点、采用的交通方式和其他变量。

4. 此外,多方式交通运输系统的有效集成是一个与多种出行方式相关的效率最大化,费用最小化的主要目标。

5. 交通系统管理的具体方面包括采用高占有率车辆优先、汽车合用方案、价格策略来控制需求和其他类似的功能。

IV. Discussions.

略。

Chapter 2

I. True or false.

1. T   2. F   3. F   4. T   5. T

II. Choose the best word or phrase to complete each statement.

1. B   2. A   3. C   4. B   5. D

Ⅲ. Translate the following sentences into Chinese.

1. 首先,由于在交通拥堵期间汽车不断排放的有害气体会导致空气污染,甚至会使全球变暖进一步恶化。

2. 同时,诸如征收高额汽车税或燃油税,其他燃料费用,或者对驾照的颁发施加更多限制条件等限制私家车使用的措施应尽量采用。

3. 例如,公路建设不仅会改变水系统的水文学结构,也会影响沿线的水质。

4. 年老者和生理缺陷者属于服务不周到的群体是由于他们不能驾驶机动车而且受到身体移动的限制他们使用公共交通系统也会受到阻碍。

5. 交通拥挤强加给出行者各种费用,如:降低速度增加出行时间;更多的耗油量和汽车磨损;重新安排旅程或者使用其他供选择交通方式的不便;从长远看还有重新安置居所和重新就业的费用。

Ⅳ. Discussions.

略。

Part Ⅱ

Chapter 3

Ⅰ. True or false.

1. T   2. T   3. F   4. F   5. T

Ⅱ. Choose the best word or phrase to complete each statement.

1. B   2. D   3. B   4. A   5. D

Ⅲ. Translate the following sentences into Chinese.

1. 在间断流的交通条件下,车辆之间的相互作用以及车辆与道路间的相互作用在确定该段交通流时发挥次要作用。

2. 高密度表示车辆个体之间的距离很近,然而低密度则意味着车辆之间的距离较远。

3. 空当是一种时间计量方法,用以表示第一辆车的后保险杠与第二辆车前保险杠的时间间隔,然而车头时距则是表示第一辆车与第二辆车的前保险杠之间的时间间隔。

4. 通常情况下通过采集该领域中速度与密度的数据,在图中描绘出这些数据点,然后通过线性回归的方法把这些数据点拟合成一条直线。

5. 在图表中,斜线表示运动中的个体车辆的轨迹,水平线则表示静止车辆。

Ⅳ. Discussions.

略。

Chapter 4

Ⅰ. True or false.

1. T   2. T   3. F   4. T   5. F

Ⅱ. Translate the following sentences into Chinese.

1. 交通控制设施是交通工程师与驾驶人进行交流的媒介。

2. 按照不同的应用目的和功能,交通标线可分为三大类:纵向标线、横向标线、物标和反光物标。

3. 交叉口信号控制的主要任务是避免交叉口发生冲突以确保驾驶人和行人安全、有效地通过交叉口。

4. 在没有交通控制的情况下即使视距在安全范围内,可能还存在其他因素需要实施更高级别的控制。

5. 因为它给特定的交通量轮流分配路权,所以比起其他的控制方式,它能够很大程度的降低交叉口冲突的数量和种类。

6. 因为它给特定的交通量轮流分配路权,所以比起其他的控制方式,它能够很大程度的降低交叉口冲突的数量和种类。

Ⅲ. Discussions.

略。

Chapter 5

Ⅰ. True or false.

1. F   2. T   3. T   4. F   5. F   6. T

Ⅱ. Translate the following sentences into Chinese.

1. 我们需要明智的规划,以环境影响最小这一合理的成本来帮助创建高质量的运输服务。失败的规划会导致严重的交通拥堵,危险的出行模式,不良的土地利用模式、不良的环境影响以及金钱和资源的浪费。

2. 未来人口预测都是建立在假设的出生率、死亡率和研究区域的迁移率上的。

3. 交通分配的确定是建立在可用的开放性土地和可实现的交通规划中的提议上的。

4. 通常土地利用规划是在交通规划前形成的,而且不会因为交通的改善而改变。

5. 出行预测模型用于预测未来交通,是决定新的道路所需通行能力,运输服务的变化和土地利用政策和模式变化的基础。

6. 重力模型使得出行基于其他小区的大小(由出行吸引力大小判断)和到其他小区的出行距离。

7. 对于公交出行,出行成本是该行程出行费用的平均出行费用,而对于小汽车出行,出行费用将在出行里程数乘以每公里成本费用的基础上增加停车费用。

8. 每组 O-D 出行随即被分配到最短路径中的各个路段,总出行数就是所有路段上的相加。分配的出行数根据每个路段的通行能力来判断是否拥堵。如果一个路段拥堵,路段上的速度则会降低而造成该路段上花费的时间变长。出行时间的变化意味着最短路径可能会改变。拥堵路段上的出行将会转移到不拥堵的路段上直到平衡,这时条件满足。

Ⅲ. Discussions.

略。

Chapter 6

I. True or false.

1. F   2. T   3. T   4. F   5. T

II. Choose the best word or phrase to complete each statement.

1. B   2. C   3. D   4. C   5. A

III. Translate the following sentences into Chinese.

1. 随着许多原先非机动化国家的机动车辆的迅速增加,每年因交通事故导致的死亡总人数也急剧增长,预计 2020 年将超过 200 万人数。

2. 在美国,由交通事故引发的受伤人数为每年 500 万人,大大超过死亡人数,这其中大多数属于轻度受伤。

3. 研究表明交通碰撞发生的风险率与车速成正比,交通引起的受伤与速度的平方成正比,交通引发的死亡与速度的 4 次方成正比。

4. 对比严重的单一车辆事故以及与交通事故无关的犯罪事件中(比如,一个典型的例子,盗窃),在性别和年龄参与事件的发生相关率显示了惊人的相似性。

5. 美国研究发现道路使用者是事故发生唯一因素的比例占 57%,道路和车辆是唯一因素的分别占 3% 和 2%;相应的英国研究估计道路使用者,道路以及车辆作为单独事故发生因素所占的比例分别为 65%、2% 和 2%。

IV. Discussions.

略。

Chapter 7

I. True or false.

1. T   2. F   3. F   4. T   5. F

II. Translate the following sentences into Chinese.

1. 在很多地方有可共享的出租车,它提供请求式服务,有的出租车要等乘客坐满后才开始运行。

2. 由于历史和经济因素,导致不同国家对公共交通的范围和使用有不同的规定。

3. 该服务可以采取多种形式、提供不同距离的服务、采用不同类型的车辆,而且可以采用固定或可变的路线和时间表。

4. 在一些不通火车的城市,长途客运非常的普遍,它作为城市长途客运的主要形式,比起铁路运输更加的灵活,且费用较低。

5. 在许多靠水的城市或岛屿,渡轮构成了公共运输系统的一部分。尽管速度很低,渡轮在点到点的直线交通中比起桥梁和隧道造价要低得多。

6. 通常,时刻表将列出车辆达到或离开特定地点的时刻。

III. Discussions.

略。

Chapter 8

I. True or false.
1. T   2. T   3. F   4. T   5. T

II. Choose the best word or phrase to complete each statement.
1. B   2. A   3. D   4. C   5. C

III. Translate the following sentences into Chinese.

1. 众多的先进出行者信息系统在今天正从有限分布的手工劳动密集型作业逐渐形成更加高度自动化并可以为出行者需求服务的流程工艺。

2. 随着各种各样的收费方式的出现以及电子收费(ETC)还远未出现时,当局确立了一种个体正式收费表,表中涉及车辆物理特性,车辆使用或者其他文化或政治因素。

3. 当某位用户注册加入电子收费系统时,该用户的车辆即被电子收费系统登记,反过来,也会给每辆车指定一种车辆类型并将该类型添加到应答器。

4. 随后,当车辆行驶在收费车道上,车道上安装的自动车辆分类系统即对车辆进行监测并使用程序指示将这些监测数据转换成一个车辆类型。

5. 由于无法检测一个点,电感线圈和逻辑算法的成功应用受到了限制。

IV. Discussions.

略。

参 考 文 献

[1] 林丽,邬岚. 交通工程专业英语[M]. 北京:中国林业出版社,2012.

[2] 刘澜编. 交通工程专业英语[M]. 成都:西南交通大学出版社,2006.

[3] 赵祖康,黄兴安. 英汉道路工程词汇[M]. 北京:人民交通出版社,2001.

[4] 胡庚申. 英语论文写作与发表[M]. 北京:高等教育出版社,2003.

[5] Roess, R. P., Prassas, E. S. and Mcshane, W. R. Traffic Engineering[M]. 4th edition. New York:Prentice-Hall, 2010.

[6] Kennedy, N., Kell, J. H. and Homburger W. S. Fundamentals of Traffic Engineering[M]. California:University of California, 1993.

[7] Hay, J. Progress in Traffic Engineering[J]. Traffic Engineering Control, 1961,3,(1):102-156.

[8] Ogden, E. The Development of Traffic Engineering in a County[J]. Highway Engingeers, 1961,(11),154.

[9] Matson, T. M., Smith, W. S., & Hurd, F. W. Traffic Engineering[M]. New York, McGraw Hill, Civil Engineering Series, 1996.

[10] Duff, J. T. Introduction to Traffic Studies[J]. Traffic Engineering Control, 1960,2,(7):98-97.

[11] Garwood, F. Sampling of Traffic. Report of Traffic Engineering Study Group [J]. Traffic Engineering Control, 1961, 2,(9):52-55.

[12] Ministry of Transport Memorandum. Memoramdum on the Design of Roads in Rural Areas [R]. Ministry of Transport Memorandum No. 780. HMSO, 1961.

[13] Hobbs, F. D. Traffic Volume Studies [J]. Traffic Engineering Control, 1960,2,(6):34-36.

[14] Williams, T. E. H., & Emmerson, J. Traffic Volumes, Journey times and Speeds by Moving Observer Method [J]. Traffic Engineering Control, 1961,3,(6):75-78.

[15] Dickson, G. M. Edinburgh region Traffic Survey[J]. Traffic Engineering Control, 1961, 3,(4):85-88.

[16] Cassie, W. F. and Jones, J. H. The Tyne Tummel:a traffic and economic study[R]. England, Department of Civil Engineering , King's College, University of Durham, 1958.

[17] Arvidsson, A. Management of Reconfigurable Virtual Path Networks[R]. ITC, 1994: 931-940.

[18] Filipiak, J. Modelling and Control of Dynamic Flows in Communication Networks[M]. Berlin: Springer Village, 1988.

[19] Gopal, G., Kim, C., and Weinrib A. Algorithms for Reconfigurable Networks[C]. Proceedings 13th International Teletraffic Congress Teletraffic and Datatraffic in a Period of Change, 1991, (18): 341-347.

[20] Pitsillides, A., Ioannou, P., and Tipper, D. Integrated Control of Connection Admission, Flow Rate, and Bandwidth for ATM Based Networks [R]. IEEE INFOCOM, 1996: 603-609.

[21] Sharma, S. and Tipper, D. Approximate Models for the Study of Nonstationary Queues and Their Applications to Communication Networks[R]. IEEE, 1993: 352-358.

[22] Shioda, S., Saito, H., and Yokoi, H. Sizing and Provisioning for Physical and Virtual Path Networks Using Self-Sizing Capability[J]. The Institute of Electronics, Information and Communication Engineers Transactions on Communications, 1997, E80-B (2): 252-262.

[23] Tanner, M. Practical Queueing Analysis[M]. England, McGraw Hill Book Company Europe, 1995.

[24] Wang, W., Tipper, D., Banerjee, S. A Simple Approximation for Modeling Nonstationary Queues[J]. IEEE INFOCOM, 1996: 201-208.

[25] Abu-Lebdeh, G. and Benekohal, R. F. Development of Traffic Control and Queue Management Procedures for Oversaturated Arterials, Transportation Research Record 1603[R], 1997:119-127.

[26] Improta, G. and Cantarella, G. E. Control Systems Design for an Individual Signalised Junction[J]. Transportation Research Board, 1984,18: 147-167.

[27] Vincent, R. A. and Young, C. P. Self-optimizing Traffic Signal Control Using Microprocessor: The TRRL "MOVA" Strategy for Isolated Intersections[J]. Traffic Engineering Control, 1986,27: 385-387.

[28] Little, J. D. C. The Synchronization of Traffic Signals by Mixed Integer Linear Programming[J]. Operation Research, 1966,14: 568-594.

[29] Gartner, N. H., Assmann, S. F., Lasaga, F. and Hom, D. L. A Multiband Approach to Arterial Traffic Signal Optimization[J]. Transportation Research Board, 1991,25: 55-74.

[30] Luk, J. Y. K. Two Traffic Responsive Area Traffic Control Methods: SCAT and SCOOT [J]. Traffic Engineering Control, 1984, (25): 14-22.

[31] Sen, S. and Head, L. Controlled Optimization of Phases at an Intersection[J]. Transportation Science, 1997,(31): 5-17.

[32] Pisarski, A. E. New Perspectives in Commuting[R]. Washington, U. S. Department of Transportation,1992.

[33] Beroldo, Stephen. Casual Carpooling in the San Francisco Bay Area[J]. Transportation Quarterly, 1990 44:(1):133-150.

[34] Wachs, Martin. Transportation for the Elderly: Changing Lifestyles, Changing Needs[M]. Berkeley: University of California Press, 1979.

附录:交通专业英语网址选编

中华人民共和国交通运输部	www.moc.gov.cn
中国铁路总公司	www.china-railway.com.cn
中国交通运输协会	www.cctanet.org.cn
中国道路运输协会	www.crta.org.cn
中国铁道学会	www.crs.org.cn
国家智能交通系统工程技术研究中心	www.itsc.com.cn
中国交通技术网	www.tranbbs.com
中华铁路网	www.chinamor.cn.net
中国交通信息	www.ictspc.gov.cn
中国交通在线	www.chinatransonline.com
中国公路网	www.highway-china.com
中国交通运输信息中心	www.365tt.com
交通技术站	www.365jt.com
BRT 中国网	www.chinabrt.org
美国交通部	www.dot.gov
日本交通部	www.mlit.go.jp
美国联邦道路管理局	www.fhwa.dot.gov
美国运输安全管理局	www.tsa.gov/public
美国运输研究学会	www.arei-online.org
加拿大运输协会	www.lma.ica.ca
美国运输研究所	www.trb.org
全球 BRT 数据库	www.brtdata.org
美国运输部运输服务中心图书馆	www.tasc.dot.gov
美国运输部国家运输图书馆	www.bts.gov/NTL
国外学位论文查询	wwwlib.umi.com/dissertations
Science Citation Index(SCI)	www.isinet.com

索　引

Accessibility	2,3,4
Acoustic	80
Acute	60
Advanced Traveller Information Systems(ATIS)	17
airline call sign	69
air terminal	4
algorithm	10,39,40,43,46,80
antagonistic	36,37,39
antiquity	61
automated toll-collection systems	6
automatic vehicle identification	16
average vehicle occupancy	4
beacon	36
behavior	50,53,57,61-63
branch-and-bound	39
car pool	52,53
cellular	76,78
charitable	60
city dwellers	13
coach	68,69
commercial vehicles	16,77
commute	3
commuter	20,69,74,75,77,83,84
commuter rail	69,84
compatible	4,37
compensation	60
conflict	59,74
congestion	2,3,9,10,11,13-17,34,48,54

	76-78
congestion pricing	14-17
consciousness	60
construction period	17
contributory	61
convert	25,53
crash	60-63
curb	6,16
damage	61,62,78
deliver	4,39,70,76
density	25-28,49,70,74
designate	25,45
devastate	60
digitalization	78
dilemma	2
disseminate	77
drunk driving	62
economic incentive	14
energy consumption	15
engineering measures	15
entrance ramp	16,36
Equilibrium	54,57
expert panel	49
external	24,34,51
facilitate	50,76
facility design	5,6
fatality	60,62,63
ferry	70
flourishing	13
flow	24-30,43,84
fluctuate	16
four step process	50
freight	4
freight transportation	16
fuel tax	16
fundamentally	13
funiculars	70
gap	25,26

geometric design	4,6
Global Positioning System (GPS)	78
gravity model	52
grieve	60
headway	25,26,54,68
hedonistic	63
heterogeneity	17
high-occupancy vehicle lanes	16
highway planning	55
highway system	3,4,51
home based trips and non-home based trips	55
households interview	55
hydrological	15
impetus	16
incrementally	3
indicator	64
inductance	80
infrared	80
in motion	29,79
in real time	16,38,79
insert	27,79
integral	76
intelligent transportation systems (ITS)	6,14
intermodal	58,76
interrupted flow	2,24,26,27,30
intersection	14,30,41,51
in-vehicle GPS and mapping systems	6
Jam Density	27,28
land parcel	3
land use	2,15,16,48-51
land-use patterns	2
levels of service	5
link and routes	55
lost time	14,37,38
magnetic	80
mandatory	46,62,63
maturity	2,14
menace	13

metropolis	13
miniaturization	78
mobility	3,15,35,48,58
mode split	50-53
monorail	69
motorized	21,60,63
multimodal planning	55
multimodal transportation systems	4
MUTCD	35
Navigational	69,77
odd-numbered	13
one-way street	6
operating period	15
optical	80
outnumber	60
out-of-vehicle time and in-vehicle time	55
overwhelmingly	60
paratransit	68,71
parking fees	16
peak-period	16
Pedestrian	4,36,51
pedestrian area	4
performance	5,9,11,12,26,40,47,59,61,62,85
per se	6
phase-based	38,39
PHF (Peak Hour Factor)	31
piezo-electric sensor	80
plate number	13
pneumatic tube	80
price mechanism	16
private car	13,14
proliferation	78
prominent	61
proximity	3
public transit stops	3
public transport	14-16,68-70
Public transportation	14,15,19,68
Quantitative	61

ramp	14
raw materials	3
real-time	10,36,38-41,49,59,66,77,83-85
regress	27
relevant	24,66
re-timing of traffic lights	16
retrieve	76
revenue load	69
ridership	54
right-of-way	35
rush time	13
satellite communities	49
self-reinforcing	2
Shockwaves	31
signal phase	42
sigset	38,39
Space Mean Speed	24
Spacing	25,26
Spectrum	76
speech technology	78
Speed	5,6,11,20,24-30,35,39,54,55 61-63,68-70,78,80
Stochastic	17
structural design	6
subsidy	72
substantially	40,43,48
Supersonic	61
supply and demand	16,54
sustainable transport	72
synthesize	81
telecommunication	81
Time Mean Speed	31
Timetable	68
traffic accidents	13,14
traffic analysis zones	55
traffic assignments	50
traffic congestion	13-16,34,48,54
traffic consensus	55

traffic control	5,6,14,34-38
traffic markings	35
traffic mode	52
traffic planning	55
traffic regulations	6,35
traffic responsive	44
traffic signals	35
traffic signs	35
traffic stream	14,29,30
traffic volume	5,15
transit	3,4,6,21,50-53
transit headways	54
transportation demand	2,34
transportation facilities	2,3
transportation mode	4
transportation planner	2
transportation systems management (TSM)	7
Travel Time	5,15,40,41
trip distribution	51,52
trip generation	50-52
trip production and trip attraction	56
unbearable	60
uninterrupted flow	24,26,27,30
urban transportation planning	50
vehicle-tracking systems	6
Victim	60
Visual	15
waiting time and transfer time	56
warrant	79
wireless communications	78